THE POETRY OF
THOMAS HARDY

edited by
Patricia Clements
and
Juliet Grindle

BARNES & NOBLE

Barnes & Noble Books
81 Adams Drive,
Totowa, N.J. 07512

ISBN 0-389-20057-3

**In memory of
J. M. Grindle**

First published in the U.S.A. 1980
© 1980 by Vision Press, London

Printed and bound in Great Britain
MCMLXXX

Barnes & Noble Critical Studies

General Editor: Anne Smith

The Poetry of Thomas Hardy

Contents

Preface

These essays were written at our invitation, and they are printed for the first time in this book. They are presented as a contribution to the renewed conversation about Hardy's poems, as part of a revaluation which must produce a more satisfying view of his complex, large, experimental, odd, rich, sometimes frustrating, compelling body of poems than it has often in the past managed to call forth from his critics. They submit Hardy's multiply personative poems to the scrutiny of eleven persons. They aim to treat the poems at once 'as poetry and not another thing' (to use a phrase T. S. Eliot wrote, though not about Hardy) and as part of their context, the products of their time and place.

The first three essays in this book deal with Hardy's craft. Isobel Grundy, Ronald Marken and S. C. Neuman set his words, and his exceptionally diverse combinations of them, in the frame of their purpose, examining the connections of technique and meaning. The next four essays locate the poems in various of their landscapes. Rosemary Eakins sets them in relation to the novels; Jeremy Steele investigates a complex fusion in some of them of Hardy's reading and his personal life; Cornelia Cook examines the exchange between Hardy and George Meredith in the context of the intellectual life of their time; and Glen Wickens considers the ways in which Hardy makes *The Dynasts* a critical and original response to the century he left behind him when he turned entirely to poetry. The final four essays trace some patterns in the poems and explore the relationships between ideas or experience and their expression in sensory language. Patricia Ingham addresses the expression in a claustrophobic imagery of Hardy's view of time; Patricia Clements sees in the shapes and style of Hardy's poems the expression of a contest between artistic order and the unruly behaviour of things; Simon Gatrell observes the purpose of his repeated figure of pilgrimage; and Jon Stallworthy reads, in an imagery of reflected light, a design of Hardy's self-revelation.

This book is indebted, as any book on Hardy's poems now must be, to Samuel Hynes and J. Hillis Miller and Donald Davie, whose work has ensured that the conversation about Hardy's poems will continue. We are grateful to them. And we are especially grateful to the contributors to this book, for joining the discussion.

We also want to thank Brian Turner, who helped in the preparation of the manuscript, and Linda Pasmore, who typed it.

P. C.
J. M. G.

Edmonton and Oxford, 1980

Editorial Note

In all of the following essays, references to Hardy's poems are given parenthetically as the numbers in *The Complete Poems of Thomas Hardy*, edited by James Gibson (London: MacMillan, 1976). References to Florence Emily Hardy, *The Life of Thomas Hardy* (London: Macmillan, 1962), are also given in the texts of the essays.

1

Hardy's Harshness

by ISOBEL GRUNDY

The first piece to confront the reader of Hardy's *Complete Poems* is 'Domicilium', a blank-verse description of his birthplace and early home which Hardy wrote before he was twenty. It is a spare and prosaic statement, from the opening ('It faces west . . .') to the close ('So wild it was when first we settled here'). If the details (remembered and reported by the writer and his now-dead grandmother) achieve a kind of dignity, they do so through their unassuming presentation, what Hardy himself later called their 'obvious and naïve fidelity'. The poet clearly implies that these things hold an importance for him which they would hold for no other, because they gave him, as a child, his personal history, his private past. No wonder he calls the poem 'Wordsworthian' (*Life*, p. 41).

Any reader who forms expectations on the basis of this poem will receive a rude shock on moving on to the second, 'The Temporary the All', which stood at the head of Hardy's first published collection of verse, *Wessex Poems*, 1898. It begins

> Change and chancefulness in my flowering youthtime,
> Set me sun by sun near to one unchosen;
> Wrought us fellowlike, and despite divergence,
>   Fused us in friendship.

Nothing could possibly be less like the straightforwardness of 'change has marked / The face of all things' ('Domicilium'). The first three words of 'The Temporary the All' sound like an arbitrary elaboration of the simple cliché 'change and chance'. Other phrases are equally open to simplifying paraphrase: 'my flowering youthtime' is an embroidered version of 'my youth' and 'sun by sun' of 'day by day'; 'despite divergence, / Fused us in friendship' suggests a mixed metaphor in which things travelling away from each other are yoked by violence together.[1] The whole

is cast in a metre of particularly outlandish sound to an English
ear, even perhaps inimical to the English language, though it
had been used to startling effect in English by Cowper and by
Swinburne.[2] When he published his *Selected Poems* in 1916
Hardy threw the reader a lifebelt in the laconic sub-title 'Sapphics'. To recognize the classical metre, however, may only add to
the unease of a reader who perceives the strong Anglo-Saxon
flavour in the emphatic alliteration and also in *forthcome, outshow*
(verbs), *breath-while, life-deed*, and *my onward earth-track*.
Other bothersome words include *intermissive*, not in any of its
OED senses ('Of the nature of, pertaining to, intermission;
intermittent; coming at intervals'), but as 'in the meantime'; and
showance in the sense of 'what there is to be shown'—a word for
which the *OED* can show only two examples, both from Hardy.
To these odd words the poem adds odd and inverted phrases
('Cherish him can I', 'Bettered not has Fate'). Of these the first
might be compelled by the metre, but Hardy has freely chosen
not to write 'Fate has not bettered', just as he chose to write
unchosen and *unformed* instead of 'not chosen' (by me) and 'not
formed'. The syntax includes the obsolete past tense and Brown-
ingesque ellipsis 'the thing sufficeth', where the sense requires
'that' or 'which'. Altogether the style does nothing to elucidate
or to smooth the poem's difficult subject, which is the way in
which the chance friend, mistress, home or career, which just
happen to present themselves, usurp the place reserved in intention for the chosen ideal. Several critics recently have relished
the oddness of this poem, and while they differ among themselves
as to whether Hardy's numerous reworkings of it tend on the
whole towards smoothing or accentuating the harshness, they
agree in finding that, unlike the life-circumstances of the poem's
speaker, this harshness was deliberately chosen.[3] Indeed, the
oddity of style and difficulty of apprehension reinforce the message
of the unexpectedness and dissatisfactions of life.

This poem can usefully stand as exemplar of the quality in
Hardy's poetry which I wish to discuss. I use the term 'harshness'
as a reminder that it is a quality not unknown in English poetry
before *Wessex Poems*. Samuel Johnson recognized it when he
wrote, 'Language suffers violence by harsh or daring figures, by
transposition, by unusual acceptations of words, and by any
licence, which would be avoided by a writer of prose' (*Idler* 77,

6 October 1759). Accurately enumerating the components of the style which Hardy was to make his own, Johnson expressed a greater respect and admiration, all other things being equal, for poetry which qualifies for his contrary term, 'easy': 'Easy poetry is that in which natural thoughts are expressed without violence to the language'. Yet Johnson, who admired force, did not prohibit even violence. In this essay he uses as one example of harshness the opening lines of Pope's *Iliad* translation, a work he deeply admired: 'the language is distorted by inversions, clogged with superfluities, and clouded by a harsh metaphor ... words are used in an uncommon sense ....' Johnson's criticism at least recognizes, as a possible road for poetry to take, that which too many critics of Hardy have assumed to be not a chosen path but an inadvertent series of lapses.[4]

Hardy's harshness in poetry was noticed from the beginning, and from the beginning commentators divided into those who attributed such 'slovenly, slipshod, uncouth verses' to 'clumsiness' and 'technical inexpertness' and those who saw them as, in Lytton Strachey's words, 'in reality an essential ingredient in the very essence of his work'.[5] The majority of academic critics for too long assumed either that Hardy would have written an 'easier' style if he had not been unfortunately incapable of it,[6] or else that he chose not to, but made a mistake in so choosing. Recent years have at last produced much sympathetic and acute analysis of Hardy's style; but I believe there is still something useful to be said.

It is important to realize that those elements which I include under the title of harshness (very new, very old, and very unusual words, periphrasis, inversion, oddities of syntax, imagery, and sound) arise out of Hardy's experimental and inventive approach to language in general. This approach declares itself in the whole stanza of proper names in 'The Peasant's Confession' (25), in the similar listing of items of a soldier's kit in 'The Alarm' (26), in the way Hardy plays on meanings in 'The Ruined Maid' (128) and plays with rhymes in 'A Refusal' (*skin burn* and *chin burn* with *Swinburne*, 778) and 'The Bridge of Lodi' (74)—which he tells us in a footnote to 'Pronounce Loddy', but which he then rhymes with *toady* and *palinody* as well as *nod he* and *trod he*. It is reflected too in his fondness for making one part of speech do the work of another, for instance his use of *vigil* and *besom* and the far more familiar *while, small, cold, east, west, lip*, and *eye*, as verbs. (He seems particularly to have liked the names of parts of the body in this form.) In 'The Sick Battle-God' (64) Hardy used the naïvely excitable diction of poetic devotees of the 'lurid Deity of heretofore': 'His crimson form, with clang and chime, / Flashed on each murk and murderous meeting-time'. To recognize Hardy's playfulness removes the objections which critics have brought against this poem. Such 'rune and rhyme' is obsolete now that 'thought outbrings / The mournful many-sidedness of things.'

In 'After Reading Psalms XXXIX, XL, etc.', Hardy based his whole poetic effect on a quirk of language—the contrast between the Latin rhymes, *fecisti, deduxisti*, etc., and the English *tryst I, missed I*, etc. The Latin, second-person-singular, perfect-tense, polysyllabic forms of active, transitive, verbs have a strength and confidence fitting the message, 'Thou hast performed, Thou hast led forth'. The English, in which the first person singular is awkwardly attached to odd nouns (*grist* as well as *tryst*) or on the wrong side of often archaic and feeble verbs (*wist, list*), feels tentative and ill at ease—yet, almost shockingly, it rhymes with the strong, confident Latin (which, again almost shockingly, looks stranded and misplaced in the English poem). By purely technical, purely linguistic means Hardy has rendered the gulf between his own and the Psalmist's thinking, and the astonishing fact that contact is made across the gulf. The meaning of the whole poem is led by the rhyme, but it is not led anywhere that it does not wish to go.

These particular oddities, suggestive as they are, may easily be overlooked as mere trivial fun, outside the mainstream of Hardy's work. Those of his linguistic idiosyncrasies which appear to arise from high spirits are most of them immediately acceptable, like 'Boney he'll come pouncing down' in 'The Sergeant's Song' (19), which is vivid and unusual without being shocking. But even his most serious and weighty poems include, in some profusion, words and expressions which strike the reader as invincibly odd, which we suppose any other poet either would not have thought of or would unhesitatingly have rejected. (We can hardly call this an admission in poetry of licence which a prose-writer would avoid, since Hardy's prose yields innumerable examples of the same effect, as when he writes of the *shortcoming* of the oldest architecture compared with geology, giving the word a far more literal meaning than is usual. *Life*, p. 94.) Often such words or expressions of Hardy's have been chosen by rejecting a much more obvious alternative. Sometimes, though rarely, the odd word comes from dialect (*blooth* for bloom, *lewth* for lee or shelter), and much more frequently from the past. Of his archaisms, many draw further attention to themselves by being especially 'literary' or 'romantic'—words which not only were out of use when Hardy wrote them but which perhaps had never been used outside a few specialized contexts. Others of his words—coinages, neologisms—had never been used at all. Some of his unusual compounds (*mindsight, wonderwork*) fit so naturally into the language that it is the very fact of their unfamiliarity that surprises; others (*subtrude, retrocede*) seem to have been picked and moulded with the express intention that they should remain nonce-words, adapted to no other user, no other occasion—though some words of which this seems to be true turn out on investigation to have been found, not invented, by Hardy. The average reader has no hope of guessing which of his words are too old and which too new to be familiar.

Often we have to pause and speculate, sometimes experience doubt and uncertainty, before lighting on Hardy's meaning, either because of a word's total unfamiliarity, or because it is more familiar in some other usage than in his recondite or unique one, or even because a specialized meaning exists which Hardy ignores. 'When the reader has overcome his surprise at discovering that "stillicide" is not a crime, he may notice the implications of whispering, muted and lone';[7] but very few readers are immune from that surprise, or able to recognize the true meaning—a steady falling of drops of water—without seeking help from a dictionary. *Embowment* is given an architectural meaning, rare and obsolete, by the *OED*; Hardy uses it generally in connection with the rainbow, once possibly with that rainbow which Noah saw;[8] this meaning may be quite easily guessed, but leaves anybody acquainted with the architectural sense slightly at a loss.

Often instead of forcing us to discover a hard or unusual meaning, Hardy makes us accept two different ones simultaneously. Commentators have noted some of his individual puns, but I believe no one has pointed out that a fondness for puns is one of his characteristics, to a degree that calls for a kind of wariness not inappropriate to approaching James Joyce. In 'His Immortality' (109) *fellow-yearsmen*, used for contemporaries, draws some of its force from the local usage of *yearsman* as 'labourer hired for the year' (*OED*). In 'Heredity' (363) *durance* suggests duration, and enduring, and imprisonment. The jumbled corpses in 'The Levelled Churchyard' (127) are 'mixed to human jam', which combines the two shock effects of frustrated movement and of cooking. 'In the Cemetery' (342), on a similar theme, has the deceived mothers weeping over 'a new-laid drain', where reminiscence of the commoner 'new-laid egg' provides a similarly nasty jolt. The 'baring bough' in 'Autumn in King's Hintock Park' (163) is being stripped by the season; the odd phrase (with adjective as verb) forces us to remember that it was lately a *bearing* bough. When in 'During Wind and Rain' (441) the 'sick leaves reel down in throngs', it is the combination of dancing with feebleness which moves us. In 'Discouragement' (811) Hardy gives a pivotal position to a double meaning when 'the Mother, naturing Nature' sees her 'hopes dismayed': a whole literary tradition of genial May feeling is turned back and frustrated. Many of the negative coinages for which Hardy is famous work in this manner: when we read 'I'd have my life unbe' in 'Tess's Lament' (141) we are not permitted to reject either the sense of 'never have existed', or that of 'be (violently) destroyed'. Titles themselves embody double meanings or distracting hints: in 'A Wasted Illness' (122) the painful approach to death has gone for nothing, been thrown away by recovery, but the full shock of this idea is held back from us for a moment by the title's similarity to the less emotive, almost technical phrase 'wasting illness'; 'Afterwards' (511) deals with words to be spoken of the poet after his death; 'The Revisitation' (152) announces that to visit the scenes of one's past is also to return like a ghost—as Hardy reminds us again in using the word *haunt* of the living ('A Trampwoman's Tragedy', 153, 'On Martock Moor', 797)—and heads a poem particularly rich in multi-meaninged phrases. Rabbits 'earthward flitting' run for their burrows, but travel also towards death. Immediately after his meditations on the ancient barrows and the plaining (and planing?) peewits, which look the same but are many generations removed from the peewits of his courtship days, the speaker describes himself as 'living long and longer / In a past that lived no more'. That is: he thinks for a long time about his dead past; he lives on and on, longer than the dying generations of peewits, and unlike them in his memory; in thinking of the ancient barrows he stretches his imaginary timespan far beyond his real one; and, as the end of the story reveals, he outlives love. In 'living long and longer . . .' Hardy distils, in a phrase in itself eminently 'easy', the essence of this whole poem. The verbal habit of double or multiple meanings, like that of difficult meanings, reflects a habit of complex thought.

Hardy can produce effects of strangeness even from ordinary and unambiguous words. Sometimes he does this by inverted or syntactically peculiar phrases, like 'could ever have mingled we' in 'At a Bridal' (6), which singles out *we* for rhyme and emphasis, or 'On which lost the more by our love' in 'Neutral Tones' (9), from which some thought may be necessary to extract the meaning 'As to which of us lost . . . .' Even in the simplest, clearest grammar, the simple facts become weird in the conclusion of 'The Duel' (379): 'He's clay, and we are free.' Hardy loves periphrases which work on the principle of a riddle, a crossword clue or an Old English kenning, to make the reader reach behind the words for the meaning. A library becomes 'a tomb of tomes', disillusioning sights are 'dream-endangering eyewounds', wrinkles are 'time-lines', love is 'pull-heart play', birds in winter 'hopping casement-comers', and Henry VIII becomes 'the much self-widowered'.[9] The unnatural habit of war provokes phrases in which certain words are clearly under strain: the noise of a battlefield is 'a miles-wide pant of pain' and casualty lists are 'the hourly posted sheets of scheduled slaughter'.[10] On some subjects Hardy has accumulated a number of periphrases, as for live and dead bodies 'wrinkled gear', 'hot carrion', 'pulseless mould'.[11] By these techniques as by his choice of single words, Hardy is able to give his reader actual difficulty in understanding. He also delights in tongue-twister effects which make speaking or reading certain lines difficult. 'To My Father's Violin' (381) mimics the difficult nimbleness of fingering in 'From your four thin threads and eff-holes came outflowing'. In 'And the May month flaps its glad green leaves like wings', the proportion of consonants to syllables (28 to 11) is abnormally high, and heavy stresses follow each other with no intervening unstressed syllables ('Afterwards'). Not only must the reader make a complete change in rhythm and movement between this and the succeeding 'Delicate-filmed as new-spun silk' (in a line with 19 consonants, 13 syllables, and stresses less heaped upon each other); he or she is also slowed and clogged as if the poem were positively resisting vocalization.

It is true that all these oddities alternate in Hardy's verse with passages of stylistic simplicity and plainness. 'That we come to live, and are called to die' ('Yell'ham-Wood's Story', 244) and 'love / All it was said to be' ('Shut Out That Moon', 164) have a breath-taking ease, and some critics have chosen to praise Hardy for these qualities exclusively, maintaining that his eccentricities of diction are confined to inferior poems, and are eschewed in some of his finest, such as 'The Oxen' and 'In Time of "The Breaking of Nations" '. This, I believe, is an untenable position: it would ignore harshness co-existing, as in 'Yell'ham-Wood's Story' and 'Shut Out That Moon', with ease; it would not only savagely restrict the number of poems deemed to have passed the test, but would leave lurking doubts about even those linguistically least exceptional of all. 'The Oxen' (403) has the localized *barton* and *coomb*, the figurative *flock* for the family, the periphrastic *strawy pen* (hardly revealed as periphrasis until we realize how surprising it is that this poem nowhere contains the word *stable*), and the odd notion of the never-questioned belief having been woven. 'In Time of "The Breaking of Nations" ' (500) has the archaic *maid* and *wight*, and also the curious image of cosmic handwriting suggested by 'War's annals will cloud into night'. Hardy's minor revisions of these poems—*would weave* for *believe, cloud* for *fade*: each, I feel, a very important improvement—address themselves to the touches of strangeness in otherwise easily accessible poems, either introducing the strangeness or making it more explicit. (Elsewhere also his revisions add strangeness rather than removing it, as in 'To the Unknown God' (151) *automatic* became *rote-restricted*.) It is not that Hardy introduces a 'hard word' resoundingly among simple ones, as Wordsworth introduces *diurnal* in 'A slumber did my spirit seal', but rather that even in his simplest pieces Hardy half-reveals quirks and roughnesses, and that—as these revisions show—he sought not to play them down but to emphasize them.

This is his harshness: odd words, and odd relations among words. Again I should like to call attention to the fact that it is a quality noted in other poets before him. Coleridge said that Donne's 'Muse on dromedary trots', and 'Wreathe[s] iron pokers into true-love knots.' Johnson asked about the Metaphysicals' thoughts a question that may have risen in readers' minds about some of Hardy's words: 'by what perverseness of industry they were ever found.'[12] Each of these great critics associates harshness with violence to the language, which seems fair enough of Hardy too. But the questions remain, is such violence a serious fault? or a venial fault? or does it serve some purpose, and if so what?

It is now less necessary than it used to be to stress that Hardy knew what he was doing, to argue against what he himself called the 'ascription to ignorance of what was really choice after full knowledge' (*Life*, p. 301). In verse as in prose he was a conscious and deliberate artist: if he chose harshness, if in revision he roughened rather than polished, it was because that was what he wanted to do. By an interesting coincidence, the first readers of his first, unpublished novel each noted in it the same quality, 'purpose' (*Life*, pp. 58–9). We possess the material, much of it offered us by Hardy himself, for insight into his literary purposes. His second wife contributed to the *Life* a note on his 'artistic inability to rest content with anything that he wrote until he had brought the expression as near to his thought as the language would allow' (p. 451, n. 1). Hardy explained his preference for rough edges: for touches of apparent carelessness and irregularity in style (pp. 105, 301–2, 384), for the later, more idiosyncratic but then less accepted work of Turner and Wagner (p. 329), for the individuality produced by a 'certain provincialism of feeling' (p. 147). He called the compound epithets used, with reminiscence of Homer, by William Barnes, 'in themselves singularly precise, often beautiful, definitions of the thing signified' despite their 'considerable divergence from the ordinary speech of the people.'[13] It is the business of art, he wrote, 'to intensify the expression of things', even to distort and disproportion reality in the interest of revealing the heart and inner meaning, which is generally invisible (*Life*, pp. 177, 228–9). In 'The Profitable Reading of Fiction', 1888, he wrote:

> Style ... can only be treatment, and treatment depends on the mental attitude of the novelist. ... A writer who is not a mere imitator looks upon the world with his personal eyes, and in his

peculiar moods; thence grows up his style, in the full sense of the term.[14]

The writer in prose or verse seeks to render what is personally and idiosyncratically visible to himself and not to others.

So the oddity of Hardy's diction is just what we might expect to go with the oddity revealed in his choice and treatment of material. His love of the bizarre, the grotesque, even the freakish, has been often remarked. As his Spirit Ironic has it, 'Life's queer mechanics chance to work out in this grotesque shape just now' (*Dynasts*, Part Second, IV, v). His mind is drawn to the extraordinary as image or symbol: the blind giant led by the dwarf; the abandoned house 'in a green landscape, like a skull on a table of dessert'; ghosts of soldiers mixing in the air like the tides below them, flocking like migrating birds yet with military precision; the psychological incongruities of 'Satires of Circumstance' or the picturesque incongruity of approaching 'multimarbled, Genova the Proud' through alleys full of washing lines; the self-denying middle-aged lovers meeting week by week for fifteen years on the edge of the weir which all the time holds the dead body of the woman's husband, the evidence that would have set them free for each other.[15] In the mystery tale 'The Three Strangers' Hardy goes out of his way to introduce oddities irrelevant to his overall effect: in the human scene the 'man of seventeen ... enamoured of his partner, a fair girl of thirty-three rolling years'; in the natural scene the 'little birds blown inside-out like umbrellas'.[16] The reader of his poems finds a wealth of oddities added to his or her experience. Some poems are entirely built up of enumerated natural oddities, like 'Night-Time in Mid-Fall' (699), where the weirdness of eels crossing dry land is clinched in 'Men's feet have felt their crawl', and 'Snow in the Suburbs' (701) in which 'Some flakes have lost their way, and grope back upward, when / Meeting those meandering down they turn and descend again,' and snow falling out of a tree 'near inurns' a sparrow. Hardy notices for us things which we might never have noticed for ourselves, like the way a contrary gust of wind seems to interrupt the tolling of a bell, as he does the less peculiar details of spring leaves, winter skies, evening hawk and nocturnal hedgehog ('Afterwards').

This poem presents the inevitable and tricky question of where, in Hardy's observations on human and non-human nature, we draw the line between the strange and the ordinary. Courtship is a continuing feature of human life, but a particular oddly-assorted couple may be unique; snow is ordinary, but its precise patterns may be odd; we think of 'the full-starred heavens that winter sees' as regularly and predictably on view, dependent though the view is on atmospheric conditions, but of the *precise* atmospheric conditions that interfere with the sound of the tolling bell as, if not unique, at least unusual. Hardy, I believe, is concerned to break down the distinctions we draw, to render the everyday strange to us, and the extraordinary ordinary, to make us see the particular in its irreplaceable reality, unblurred by any degree of familiarity either with the general conditions which have produced it or with any other comparable particulars.[17] In 'On the Esplanade' (682) he meticulously describes a strange, complex visual effect of moonlight on water and sums up, not without irony, 'All this, so plain'. He sets out, as he says in his 'Apology' to *Late Lyrics and Earlier*, to defy his public's expectations, infringe its prohibitions, and 'state all that crosses his mind concerning existence in this universe'. He shows us life itself as an astonishing manifestation and consciousness as more astonishing still, and he convinces us of both the rarity and the value of a poet who will 'notice such things'.

Some of those who have patronized or condescended to Hardy have managed to do so by fastening on either the ordinariness or the strangeness in his writings, while ignoring the opposing and complementary quality. If we recognize his purpose and artfulness, the unity of his work, then we must give full weight to both these elements and pay attention to the relationship between them. Again Hardy's own comments are helpful. In an early notebook he wrote, 'Though a good deal is too strange to be believed, nothing is too strange to have happened'.[18] He was always aware of the need for fiction to gratify the love of the uncommon, while remaining close enough to the reader's own experience to 'illude'—an unusual word which Hardy, characteristically, uses in a sense not recorded by *OED* (*Life*, pp. 150, 152). The reader's time must not be taken up 'with what he can get at first hand anywhere around him' (p. 362)—but what is personal in the writer's vision, even of the most ordinary things, will be exactly what the reader cannot get at first hand. In a late notebook he copied from the *Literary Supplement*, 'To extract a magic out of the familiar.'[19] The following year he copied from Emerson, 'The foolish man wonders at the unusual, but the wise man at the usual', and this quotation he recorded in the *Life* (p. 426).

Again and again, often through the oddity of their phrasing, Hardy's poems offer the reader the experience of wonder at the usual. 'A Commonplace Day' (78) is held under the microscope as 'this diurnal unit', in which the domestic ritual of pulling the fire to pieces at bedtime takes on a fearsome suggestion of extinguishing life. The easy-styled 'To Lizbie Browne' (94), about the moving power of entirely ordinary beauty, forecasts the poet's death in the ominous strangeness of 'When on a day / Men speak of me / As not'. In 'A Broken Appointment' (99) the painful recognition with which the waiting lover hears the hour strike can be heard in the harsh phrase 'the hope-hour stroked its sum'. The indefinables of delirium are captured as 'webby waxing things and waning things' in 'A Wasted Illness' (122).

'Exeunt Omnes' (335) begins 'Everybody else, then, going, / And I still left where the fair was?' The question suggests a dazed speaker only just awakening to his situation. The reader quickly realizes that the fair is an image of life itself, from which people depart 'Into the clammy and numbing night-fog / Whence they entered hither. / Soon one more goes thither!' These opening and closing lines employ easy diction, natural words in natural order, though with elliptical syntax. The middle stanza, on the contrary, moves through ease to harshness:

> There is an air of blankness
> In the street and the littered spaces;
> Thoroughfare, steeple, bridge and highway
>   Wizen themselves to lankness;
>   Kennels dribble dankness.

Of this the last line is hard to enunciate; the image preceding it describes a process hard to grasp as performed by the string of concrete nouns which make up the townscape of the fair, though it has a disturbing applicability to the human body, which helps to bring out the strangeness of the poem's central image. Life, receding, becomes less a gift to regret than a conundrum unsolved.

'Just the Same' (650) is another poem which frames a deceptive harshness with a beginning and end of extreme stylistic ease:

> I sat. It all was past;
> Hope never would hail again;
> Fair days had ceased at a blast,
> The world was a darkened den.
>
> The beauty and dream were gone,
> And the halo in which I had hied
> So gaily gallantly on
> Had suffered blot and died!
>
> I went forth, heedless whither,
> In a cloud too black for name:
> —People frisked hither and thither;
> The world was just the same.

Douglas Brown, comparing this with the three stanzas of *In Memoriam* which end 'On the bald street breaks the blank day', hovers uneasily between praise and blame: Hardy lacks verbal assurance, even verges on incompetence; his grief is smaller than Tennyson's, yet his 'infelicitous language sounds a deeper music.'[20] In fact Hardy has chosen not to force a meaning or explanation on his experience but to let his contradictions of language reveal its strangeness. 'I sat' has a frozen disquiet which neither 'I flung myself down in despair' nor 'I sat brooding for hours' could attain. The comprehensive 'It all was past' is equally vague in message, though its mood is instantly recognizable to us all. In the second line *hail* presumably means *greet*—the intransitive usage not sanctioned by that of other writers or speakers—but it becomes disturbingly associated with *blast* in the third line, suggesting a meteorological and surely uncomfortable sense, and with *halo* in the second stanza. 'Fair days' awkwardly jolts the memory of the reader of 'Exeunt Omnes', published eight years earlier. A gush of feeling emerges in the alliterative 'darkened den' and is further romanticized in 'gaily gallantly', 'hied' and 'suffered blot'. The nature of the transformation described becomes less rather than more clear: is it a movement out of or into delusion? Which view of the world, if any, is accurate? The speaker has exchanged a halo for an equally enveloping black cloud; first he sits, perceiving the world as once bright, now dark; then he goes forth, and perceives it as after all 'just the same'. Of this 'easy' phrase, which gives this poem its title and forms a recurrent thought in Hardy's poetry (the burden of 'Afterwards', 'In Time of "The Breaking of Nations"', 'A Wasted Illness' and 'Nature's Questioning', 43), we cannot say with certainty whether it contradicts or reinforces the harshness of 'darkened den' and 'suffered blot and died'. Nor can we tell whether *frisked* (an easy word, but harsh in its incongruity with the mood of the rest, and indispensable in the poem's total effect) reflects other people's innocent pleasure or culpable frivolity, or perhaps the speaker's sourness. (There is, I think, less doubt about 'the prancing folk' in 'Lines to a Movement in Mozart's E-Flat Symphony', 388). In 'Just the Same' human feeling bursts, flows, ebbs; the world remains the same in a mantle of incomprehensibility. For this reader at least, the poem brings together vividness of emotion with obscurity of interpretation, ease of feeling with impossibility of understanding, and in accomplishing this effect its strangeness of diction is crucial.

The physical world is to Hardy no more easily understood than is human emotion. In 'Nature's Questioning' in his first published collection, the things of nature ask—or rather, 'Upon them stirs in lippings mere'—the question of the reason for their existence. The word *lippings*, however apt it might be for a human being still faintly mouthing a question first clearly put a long time ago, is positively perverse as applied to the 'dawning, pool, / Field, flock, and lonely tree'; it can be accepted only to the degree that Hardy has succeeded in investing these things, which 'All seem to gaze at me / Like chastened children sitting silent in a school; / Their faces dulled, constrained, and worn,' with an aspect of strangeness as blank as that of Wordsworth's 'tree, of many, one' which told him that the old illumination was gone. (They may remind us, too, of the same poet's 'single sheep, and the one blasted tree' of another experience of mystery.)[21] The various hypotheses for existence raised in the 'lippings mere'—jest, unconsciousness, gradual running-down or imperceptible progress—are abstract and uninspiring, the mode of thought in which they are presented hardly appropriate to the chilly and precise 'Field, flock, and lonely tree'. Yet both parts of the poem are true to our experience: the existence of particulars

does raise the question *why* they exist. In transferring the question
from his own mind to the mute world's imagined lips, Hardy has
allowed neither strangeness nor familiarity to escape:

> Thus things around. No answerer I . . . .
>   Meanwhile the winds, and rains,
>   And Earth's old glooms and pains
> Are still the same . . . .

The unusual could not provoke such uneasy wonder as this.

One of the last poems that Hardy worked on, revising it on
the fifteenth anniversary of his first wife's death and only six
weeks before his own, though he had drafted it fifty years earlier,
was another on the unpredictable behaviour of nature, 'An
Unkindly May' (825).[22] The title contains a pun, familiar to us
as a favourite of many poets before Hardy. The poem begins and
ends with a shepherd who, in the easiest language, 'stands by a
gate in a white smock-frock: / He holds the gate ajar, intently
counting his flock.' The central section, by contrast, uses con-
voluted, excruciating language to enumerate the abnormalities
of the season, in which trees 'creak like rusty cranes' and familiar
pigeons and rooks look 'like gaunt vultures', and finally to record
an oddly reassuring dialogue between the poet and all this:

> The sun frowns whitely in eye-trying flaps
> Through passing cloud-holes, mimicking audible taps.
> 'Nature, you're not commendable to-day!'
> I think. 'Better to-morrow!' she seems to say.

Through it all the shepherd still stands 'Unnoting all things save
the counting his flock.' He is not wise enough to wonder at such
a mundane thing as the weather, and nor, probably, are we; we
need the noticing eye of this most peculiar poet.

For his purpose of seeking to make us wonder at the usual,
Hardy's harshness of style is invaluable. Words coined or adapted
extraordinarily for a particular occasion (the kind of thing that
made Henry Newbolt complain that he 'abuses the inventor's
privilege . . . making these words deny their ancestry and relations
for the sake of some small temporary emergency')[23] remind us
of discrepancy between past history and present occurrence, as
do so many of Hardy's fictional plots. Puns remind us of the
ambiguity of experience; odd phrases call attention both to the

uniqueness of the sensibility which has shaped them and to the little it can do to ensure our comprehension. Lines pronounced with difficulty reflect the more than simply verbal difficulties that attend the discovery and expression of truth. The idiosyncrasies of Hardy's poetic style are perfectly fitted to convey a sense of the anomalous position, in his view, of consciousness in a universe of nescient striving forces.

NOTES

1 Paul Zietlow provides a most useful analysis of this poem's language in his *Moments of Vision, The Poetry of Thomas Hardy* (Cambridge, Mass., 1974), pp. 26-7, 32-5. This is not the only instance in which Zietlow's view of Hardy's poetry resembles my own; my ideas were formed before I read his book, which I have found equally rewarding both where I agree with it and where I do not.

2 Cowper in 'Lines Written during a Period of Insanity', *c.* 1774 (*Poetical Works*, ed. H. S. Milford, corr. Norma Russell, repr. 1967, pp. 289-90); Swinburne in 'Sapphics' in *Poems and Ballads*, 1865 (*Complete Works*, ed. Sir E. Gosse and T. J. Wise, 1925-27, i. 333-35). Hardy's poem was probably influenced by Swinburne's example. Zietlow prints its first and last stanzas with prosodic markings (p. 34).

3 Kenneth Marsden, *The Poems of Thomas Hardy, A Critical Introduction* (1969), pp. 203-5; Henry Gifford in *Agenda*, x (1972) p. 128; Zietlow, pp. 32-5; James Richardson, *Thomas Hardy, The Poetry of Necessity* (1975), pp. 15-16, 93.

4 Zietlow calls 'harsh' the same elements of Hardy's style as I do—clogging or jarring sounds, heavy alliteration, grotesque coinage, 'a contrived violence of language', he opposes 'harsh' to 'prosaic', and sometimes classes as 'prosaic' poems in which I find the element of harshness important, though not dominant (pp. 243-45).

5 *Thomas Hardy, The Critical Heritage*, ed. R. G. Cox (1970), pp. 319-24, 436.

6 E. g. Donald Davie, *Thomas Hardy and British Poetry* (1973), pp. 24-5.

7 Marsden, p. 157, of 'Friends Beyond'.

8 F. B. Pinion finds this second implication in 'To Outer Nature' (*A Commentary on the Poems of Thomas Hardy*, 1976, p. 21); the word occurs also in 'On a Fine Morning' and 'Lady Vi'.

9 See poems 150, 65, 362, 536, 162, 307.

10 See poems 24 and 58.

11 See poems 336, 160, 166.

12 Coleridge, 'On Donne's Poetry'; Johnson, 'Life of Cowley', para. 55.

13 Review, 1879: *Personal Writings*, ed. H. Orel (1967), p. 96.

14 *Ibid.*, p. 122.

15 *Life*, p. 114; 'The Souls of the Slain' (62); 'Genoa and the Mediterranean' (65); 'The Waiting Supper', 1887, in *Life's Little Ironies and A Changed Man*, ed. F. B. Pinion (1977).

16 *Wessex Tales and A Group of Noble Dames*, ed. F. B. Pinion (1977), p. 15.

17 Here I differ absolutely from Donald Davie, who holds that Hardy gives no 'sign of that determination to render the particular scene, experience, or topic in all its particularized quiddity' (p. 118).

18 1871: *Thomas Hardy's Notebooks*, ed. Evelyn Hardy (1955), p. 35.

19 28 June 1923: *Notebooks*, p. 100.

20 *Thomas Hardy* (1954), pp. 171–73.

21 'Ode on the Intimations of Immortality', line 51; *Prelude*, xii, 319.

22 Drafted 1877; revised 27 November 1927 (*Life*, p. 444).

23 Review of *The Dynasts in Critical Heritage*, p. 386, n. 1.

2

'As Rhyme Meets Rhyme' in the Poetry of Thomas Hardy

by RONALD MARKEN

The second poem in Hardy's last volume of poetry, *Winter Words in Various Moods and Metres*, 'Proud Songsters' (816) is disarming in its simplicity. To the reader already familiar with Hardy's 'full look at the worst', the poem's first stanza is characteristically cautionary. Night is falling, spring is passing, and still the birds sing as though they had all the time in the world; but, he concludes, with a similarly characteristic tenderness, they are very young:

> The thrushes sing as the sun is going,
> And the finches whistle in ones and pairs,
> And as it gets dark loud nightingales
>   In bushes
> Pipe, as they can when April wears,
>   As if all Time were theirs.
>
> These are brand-new birds of twelve-months' growing,
> Which a year ago, or less than twain,
> No finches were, nor nightingales,
>   Nor thrushes,
> But only particles of grain,
>   And earth, and air, and rain.

A variety of effects reinforces the poet's diction and imagery to add to this sombre poem an accumulating and odd sense of cool spaciousness. The enjambement of stanza one (11. 3–5), for example, intensifies the straining of time against song, while Hardy intrudes the brief, almost comic fourth line, 'In bushes', between the nightingales and their less-than-dignified noise, 'pipe'. The impact of that verb is abrupt and disquietingly shrill. Hardy increases the suspense by withholding all rhyme for five

full lines, yet, adding a concluding couplet, BB, he finishes with
a six-line stanza in which half the lines rhyme. The lines of the
second stanza, on the other hand, are repeatedly silenced by
caesuras and the consequent hesitation of spaced, open vowels:
'only particles of grain, / And earth, and air, and rain.'[1] The
implications grow vaster as the images become, literally, more
particular, more elemental, more harmonious. Chromatically,
both stanzas are harmonized by the soft *ai*'s and *r*'s of 'pairs',
'wears', 'theirs', 'twain', 'grain', 'earth', 'air', and 'rain'. Similar
blending of vowels and consonants can be found in the throbbing
eleventh line of another and earlier poem, 'I Look Into My
Glass' (52)—'And shakes this fragile frame at eve'—or in the
wintry 'blown', 'moan', 'alone', 'alone' rhymes of 'The Seasons
of Her Year' (125).

   The rhyme of 'Proud Songsters' cooperates with Hardy's other
techniques and provides a solid frame for the whole. In the first
place the rhyme-scheme is unique: ABCDBB AECDEE.[2] In
addition to the A, C, and D links between the stanzas, the B and
E rhymes are assonantally similar. In a poem about heedless
youth, love and death, Hardy has taken pains to couple sound
and sense, thereby giving both rhyme and message an appropriate
inevitability.

   I once read this poem to a class of undergraduates who had
been studying prosody. Two of their responses are worth remarking in this context. Several students were actually startled by the
unexpected brevity of line four, having been lulled into thinking
that the lyrical, duple-triple metres of the first three lines would
carry on, uncurtailed. Furthermore, once they caught the rhyme-
scheme of stanza one and its early echoes in stanza two, perceptive
students were able to anticipate correctly the ending of line nine,
all of line ten, and the last two words of the poem. Such readers
initially feel like the poet's anonymous accomplices; then, they
learn to appreciate the way Hardy has 'rhymed', as it were, love
and certain death in an inexorable pattern of sound. The poem
is simple only to the heedless. The rhyme-scheme of 'Proud
Songsters' transcends its function as mere structural artifice and
becomes a meaningful instrument of premonition.

   'News for Her Mother' (206) is an inconclusive poem, but its
rhymes are also prophetic. The hurrying dimeters carry the
thoughts of a girl, anxiously returning to her mother with news

of her marriage. Will the news 'sunder / Her from me?' she worries. The question is not answered, as the poem stops before the girl reaches her mother. The rhyme, however, reveals what the poem does not say. Stanza one includes 'Mother mine . . . Apples fine . . . be as wine'; stanza two, equally optimistic, '. . . that I bound . . . along the ground.' Stanza three is anxious: 'Silly soul . . . small . . . hearts made whole.' Division shows in the fourth stanza: 'Her from me? . . . His I'd be,' and the portents of stanza five are decidedly gloomy: 'Ever bar . . . seem afar'. 'Bar-afar'—mother and daughter will not, in all likelihood, be reconciled. All twenty-nine stanzas of 'The Flirt's Tragedy' (160) end with that poem's single rhyming sound, $\overline{oo}$. No rhyme words are repeated, so Hardy exploits an extraordinary, sometimes strained parade, including 'knew', 'yew', 'purlieu', 'do', 'retinue', 'pew', 'rendezvous', 'mew', but they chime inexorably toward the tragedy of 'slew', the last word of all. More finely wrought is the subtle graduation of rhyme-sounds in the last three stanzas of 'His Immortality' (109): excelled > then > thin > mannikin > chill > still. After a penultimate 'feeble spark', the poem closes like a coffin on the word 'dark'; and there is no escaping it.

In 'A Broken Appointment' (99), Hardy is at his finest:

> You did not come,
> And marching Time drew on, and wore me numb.—
> Yet less for loss of your dear presence there
> Than that I thus found lacking in your make
> That high compassion which can overbear
> Reluctance for pure lovingkindness' sake
> Grieved I, when, as the hope-hour stroked its sum,
> You did not come.
>
> (Stanza I)

If there is suspense between the nightingales and their pipe in 'Proud Songsters', the four lines that withhold both subject and verb in this stanza's second sentence build an excruciating crescendo of tension. One reads 'Grieved I', gasping, and, although there are still small shreds of promise in 'hope-hour', the enveloping A-rhyme of 'sum' recalls the fateful 'numb'. 'You did not come' reiterates and seals the speaker's grief. Similar knells of inevitability accumulate in the rhymes of 'Long Plighted' (105) or 'Exeunt Omnes' (335), with the latter's added force of mournful, falling rhythms and feminine rhymes.

Two-thirds of the way through the stanza that stands two-thirds of the way through 'In Front of the Landscape' (246), Hardy pivots the poem on a short crux-line, 'Yea, as the rhyme'. I suggest that it is more than coincidence that places that word, 'rhyme', in such a structurally sensitive spot. In each of its twelve sestets, 'In Front of the Landscape' alternates long, metrically irregular lines ('What were the re-creations killing the daytime' 1. 17) with rhythmic, trochee-iamb dimeter ('As by the night' 1. 18; 'Harrowed by wiles' 1. 24). Furthermore, the long lines never rhyme. The dimeter lines, however, lace the stanzas together, rhyming lines two and six of each stanza with line three of the preceding stanza. Stanzas one to three, for example, are joined thus:

I   x A x B x A
         / \
II   x B x C x B
         / \
III   x C x D x C
         / \

One reads, therefore, prosaic lines alternating with rhythmical lines, with the growing expectation that the latter will find rhyming mates. Each fourth line becomes an important structural link, through rhyme, with the next stanza.

The poem's first eight stanzas describe the speaker's imaginary landscape, peopled with the forms and voices of the dead; the real vista is 'Blotted to feeble mist'. The last four stanzas summarize the speaker's feelings, his regrets:

> —Yea, as the rhyme
> Sung by the sea-swell, so in their pleading dumbness
> Captured me these.
>
> (Stanza IX)

One important aspect of these lines anticipates a function of Hardy's use of rhyme that I will discuss more fully below: the 'rhyming' of the internal universe with the external. For the moment, I call attention to Hardy's self-conscious, deliberately crucial employment of the word 'rhyme' in this stanza—and this is not an isolated example, as I will show shortly.

The landscape before him, the 'sweet, sad, sublime' (l. 60) images in his mind's eye, Hardy closes the poem by imagining what people must be saying who do not see what he sees:

> Hence wag the tongues of the passing people, saying
>   In their surmise,
> 'Ah—whose is this dull form that perambulates, seeing nought
>   Round him that looms
> Withersoever his footsteps turn in his farings . . .?'

What is the next line? How does the poem end? The rhyme-scheme obliges us to expect a line like 'With staring eyes', or something similar, to satisfy 'surmise'. But no; the poem is finished. More linking rhymes would be pointless. Hardy, therefore, seals it with an unprecedented and resonant coupling: 'looms . . . Save a few tombs.' It is not a shocking finale, but it is powerfully apt. 'He knew,' says Hardy of himself in his *Life*:

> . . . that in architecture cunning irregularity is of enormous worth, and it is obvious that he carried on into verse, . . . the Gothic art-principle in which he had been trained—the principle of spontaneity, . . . resulting in the unforeseen (as he called it) character of his metres and stanzas, . . . poetic texture rather than poetic veneer . . . .

Among the dead faces which Hardy's memory recalls in front of the landscape are:

> Some as with smiles,
> Some as with slow-born tears that brinily trundled
> Over the wrecked
> Cheeks that were fair in their flush-time, ash now with anguish,
> Harrowed by wiles.

One hears echoes here of the bruised memories of 'During Wind and Rain' (441): 'Down their carved names the rain-drop ploughs.' Time and again, the rhymes slide like drops through a Hardy poem, subtly altering its face as they move to hang on the last word like a pendant that glitters, falls, or dissolves. Often their chords are doom-laden, filled with remorse or regret.

'Amabel' (3) is such a poem. The third line of each of the eight quatrains rhymes with the repeated name of the lost love,

'Amabel'. We hear 'knell', 'Swell', 'no more tell', 'fell', in tolling reverberations that almost redeem the melodramatic finale:

> Till the Last Trump, farewell,
> O Amabel!

A similar cadence of regret informs the more successful 'To Lizbie Browne' (94), each stanza being banded by the twice-repeated lost name. The fifth stanza is the best, where 'Love' is wrung, almost like a gasp, from the last line:

> Ay, Lizbie Browne,
> So swift your life,
> And mine so slow,
> You were a wife
> Ere I could show
> Love, Lizbie Browne.

The lines are short, terminal caesuras are typical, so when 'show' runs into 'Love', the effect is one of great poignancy. The accents of remorse are also to be found in the repeated rhymes and phrases of 'Tess's Lament' (141)—'And now he's gone; and now he's gone; . . . / And now he's gone'—'The Man With a Past' (458)—'And froze like a spell— / Like a spell'—or 'If It's Ever Spring Again' (548).

This latter poem, subtitled 'Song', is spendidly musical, and Hardy uses a rhyme-scheme of extraordinary density to surround the memory of love with bittersweet abundance. Not only does he cram seven A-rhymes into each single stanza, but several of them are duple or triple rhymes, including not just the last syllable of the line but the penultimate and even antepenultimate syllables.

If it's ever spring again,	A
Spring again,	A
I shall go where went I when	A
Down the moor-cock splashed, and hen,	A
Seeing me not, amid their flounder,	B
Standing with my arm around her;	B
If it's ever spring again,	A
Spring again,	A
I shall go where went I then,	A

If it's ever summer-time,	C
Summer-time,	C
With the hay crop at the prime,	C
And the cuckoos—two—in rhyme,	C
As they used to be, or seemed to,	D
We shall do as long we've dreamed to,	D
If it's ever summer-time,	C
Summer-time,	C
With the hay, and bees achime.	C

One cannot help remarking that the couplets in the middle of each stanza are more than rhymed pairs of lines. They are, fittingly, the only lines to speak of the loving couple, almost hidden 'amid the flounder' of the mating moor-fowl and nature's other juices and joys. In the second stanza, Hardy makes it explicit: in their couplets, the lovers, like the cuckoos, are 'two—in rhyme'. He both says it and embodies it; form and meaning are one.

Each stanza is, furthermore, a single conditional sentence. The memory and the music are unbroken, while the 'If' tunes the music of his song to a distinctly minor key. Not only will the metaphorical spring and summer never return, the all-but-extinguished image of the lovers, the repetitions, and the density of rhymes makes the tone haunting, wistful, deeply sad, as they did in 'Amabel' and 'Tess's Lament'.

In the poems discussed so far, Hardy has used the principles of rhyme in several ways. The mere presence of rhyme is ingenious and satisfying in 'Proud Songsters', somewhat less so in 'The Flirt's Tragedy', and disastrous in 'To Outer Nature' (37).[3] Because rhymes fall, usually, at line endings, rhetorically susceptible spots, they give increased emphasis to the words and images in them—the 'numb' of 'A Broken Appointment' being a case in point. One might also note here the boldly defiant finale of 'I Said to Love' (77) in which the expected ABBACCA swells to ABBBACCCA:

> 'Depart then, Love! . . .
> —Man's race shall perish, threatenest thou,
> Without thy kindling coupling-vow?
> The age to come the man of now
> Know nothing of?—

We fear not such a threat from thee;
We are too old in apathy!
Mankind shall cease.—So let it be,'
    I said to Love.

The heartfelt subject-matter of much of Hardy's poetry is, as it were, made simultaneously bearable and more intense because of the rigid, even ceremonious formality and aesthetic distance his rhyming imparts. By thus framing his poems, he enables them to stand alone, part of the poetic experience of every reader. As well, he compels his rhymes to chant and build toward strains of unspoken anxiety, impending fate, so that the rhymes *per se* make meaning.

The combination of all these forces brings the discussion to Hardy's most impressive and moving exploitations of his rhyming skills in poems that mingle memory and desire, and in those that wed the landscapes of the heart and mind with those of the external universe.

'The Ballad-Singer' (194), a cross-rhymed poem of three stanzas, concludes:

Rhyme, Ballad-rhymer, start a country song;
Make me forget that she whom I loved well
Swore she would love me dearly, love me long,
    Then—what I cannot tell!

Sing, Ballad-singer, from your little book;
Make me forget those heart-breaks, achings, fears;
Make me forget her name, her sweet sweet look—
    Make me forget her tears.

'Rhyme, . . . Make me forget'. The song is an agonizing one, and the pain is intensified by irony: rhyme makes one *remember*. Here, of course, Hardy is using 'rhyme' as a verb—to act like a poet. But, just as rhymed poetry has this mnemonic effect, so too do the 'rhyming' associations of places or things generate reverberations of memory. See, for example, 'She Revisits Alone the Church of Her Marriage' (596):

Where touched the check-floored chancel
    My knees and his?
The step looks shyly at the sun,
And says, ' 'Twas here the thing was done . . . .'   (ll. 10–13)

A better, and more rending instance may be seen in 'Penance' (589):

> 'Why do you sit, O pale thin man,
>   At the end of the room
> By that harpsichord, built on the quaint old plan?
>   —It is cold as a tomb . . . .'   (Stanza I, 1–4)

> 'Why do I? Alas, far times ago
>   A woman lyred here
> In the evenfall; one who fain did so
>   From year to year . . . .'   (Stanza II, 1–4)

> 'I would not join. I would not stay,
>   But drew away,
> Though the winter fire beamed brightly . . . . Aye!
>   I do to-day
> What I would not then; and the chill old keys,
>   Like a skull's brown teeth
>   Loose in their sheath,
> Freeze my touch; yes, freeze.'   (Stanza III)

The first stanza begins almost suddenly, asking a question couched in images of chill age. In stanza two, the protagonist answers, as though from a sepulchre of guilt. The rhyme, ABABCDDC, also appears to have stiffened. In stanza three, the speaker's memory of neglect and estrangement admits to being tormented by the tangible, freezing presence of the dead past in the object under his hand. As the pain builds, so do rhyme and other figures of intense reiteration. No longer cross-rhymed, the stanza grows monosyllabic and tightens to 'stay', 'away', 'Aye', 'to-day', concluding with the piercing assonance of 'keys', 'teeth', 'sheath', 'freeze'—this latter word opening and closing the final line. The cold is profound, zero at the bone. Other sonic effects amplify the remorse: 'I would not' is thrice-repeated; 'chill', 'old', 'skull', and 'Loose' have a rattling consonance that amounts to internal rhyme. 'Penance' becomes, then, a poem about the speaker's internal rhymes of association.

The seasons can have effects as vivid as those generated by objects:

579 The Rift
(Song: Minor Mode)

'Twas just at gnat and cobweb-time,
When yellow begins to show in the leaf,
That your old gamut changed its chime
From those true tones—of span so brief!—
That met my beats of joy, of grief,
    As rhyme meets rhyme.

So sank I from my high sublime!
We faced but chancewise after that,
And never I knew or guessed my crime . . . .
Yes; 'twas the date—or nigh thereat
Of the yellowing leaf; at moth and gnat
    And cobweb-time.

At a specific time of the year, she changed her 'true tones' to jarring ones, and he never knew why. Her joys once met his, 'as rhyme meets rhyme'; now the grief of their alienation is forever rhymed with the time of gnat, cobweb, and autumn. 'Rhyme' is rhymed with five of the twelve lines, consolidating the tight structure of his recollection: ABABBA ACACCA. 'The beauty of association,' says Hardy, ' is entirely superior to the beauty of aspect, and a beloved relative's old battered tankard to the finest Greek vase. Paradoxically put, it is to see beauty in ugliness' (*Life*, pp. 120–21).

What Tom Paulin calls stark images 'can become fixed in the memory and hold intense experiences connected with them. Each image becomes the experience and this means that the mind has the power to select and retain images.' Earlier, discussing Hardy in the context of Ruskin and the pathetic fallacy, Paulin cites a note Hardy made in August, 1865: 'The poetry of a scene varies with the minds of the perceivers. Indeed it does not lie in the scene at all.' Paulin maintains, and proves, that 'this brief and unemphatic note, made at a time of increasing melancholy, states an attitude which is at the centre of all his work.'[4] The perceiver finds, makes, or is given a scene with which he has some emotional rapport. The connections may be arbitrary, paradoxical, or

apt—see 'The Seasons of Her Year', 'At Castle Boterel' (292),
'The Phantom Horsewoman' (294)—but the poet articulates
them. Hardy recorded an abridged quotation from De Quincey's
essay on style in his literary notes, observing that 'the problem
before the writer' of meditative poetry is:

> ... to pass through a prism & radiate into distinct elements what
> previously had been even to himself but dim & confused ideas
> intermixed with each other .... The skill with which detention
> or conscious arrest is given to the evanescent, external projection
> to what is internal, *outline to what is fluxionary* & body to what
> is vague ... depends on the command over language.[5]

Conscious arrest is given to the evanescent love of the woman
speaking in 'Under the Waterfall' (276):

> 'Whenever I plunge my arm, like this,
> In a basin of water, I never miss
> The sweet sharp sense of a fugitive day
> Fetched back from its thickening shroud of gray.
>> Hence the only prime
>> And real love-rhyme
>> That I know by heart,
>> And that leaves no smart,
> Is the purl of a little valley fall
> About three spans wide and two spans tall ....'

There are no intrinsic qualities in the cold water that make it
generate thoughts of love inevitably. It might as easily have been
the smell of burning pine needles, the sound of rain on a slate
roof, or a certain slant of light. The emotional turbulence in force
while such external sensations are happening can, without fail
and permanently ('I never miss'), couple the two hitherto unrelated phenomena.

The auditor of the story in 'Under the Waterfall', in fact, is
mystified by the speaker's little ritual. Her tone is teasing:

> And why does plunging your arm in a bowl
> Full of spring water, bring throbs to your soul?

(There is even gentle mockery in the rhyme of 'bowl' and 'soul'.)
The answer is familiar to Hardy's readers. She and her lover
'sipped lovers' wine' beside a tiny waterfall, and, while she rinsed

their common 'chalice', it fell into the pool under the waterfall, too deep for them to recover it, although they tried 'with long bared arms'. The vessel is still there.

Four times in the poem, Hardy uses the word 'rhyme' to speak of the sound of the waterfall, and in three of those instances it is an explicit *love*-rhyme. The poem is composed throughout in couplets, paired verses. The woman's feelings are also paired: the inside with the outside, present with past, natural with human—even natural with artificial (see ll. 43–6). And, although the poem does not say so explicitly, there is in it a melancholy suggestion that more than the wine-glass has been lost. Her lover, too, has probably slipped past recall. Why else would she place such store in this everyday water sensation? Why else is the imagery and diction so fraught with loss, death, and finality? Why else is her chilled, cold arm the '*only* prime' and '*real* love-rhyme'?

The aggrieved or regretful lovers in Hardy's love-poetry repeatedly find echoes of their aching hearts in the associative world about them. ' "*There are many echoes* in the world" ', Hardy wrote in his literary notes, quoting an unidentified 'great German poet', ' "but few voices" '.[6] One of the persistent echoes in the world of the older Hardy, and an echo to which he has given voice in some of the most eloquent love poetry in the language, is that of his dead wife, Emma:

285 The Voice

Woman much missed, how you call to me, call to me,
Saying that now you are not as you were
When you had changed from the one who was all to me,
But as at first, when our day was fair.

Can it be you that I hear? Let me view you, then,
Standing as when I drew near to the town
Where you would wait for me: yes, as I knew you then,
Even to the original air-blue gown!

Or is it only the breeze, in its listlessness
Travelling across the wet mead to me here,
You being ever dissolved to wan wistlessness,
Heard no more again far or near?

Thus I; faltering forward,
Leaves around me falling,
Wind oozing thin through the thorn from norward,
And the woman calling.

Seldom has any poet used the plaintive possibilities of falling dactylic metres to finer advantage, and the triple feminine rhymes, when they work, are plangent: 'call to me, call to me', 'all to me'. (There is a constricting awkwardness in the double vowelling of '*view you*, then,' which is, for me, the poem's only flaw.) The open, mourning vowels of 'call' and 'all' meld into a pained, diminishing *e* that echoes through each of the first three stanzas: 'hear', 'near', 'me', 'breeze', 'mead', 'here', 'near'. Even the masculine rhymes of the shorter, hypercatalectic lines are not abrupt; they fade away into delicate *r*'s and *n*'s. In the third stanza, as the vision begins to disappear, the wind's voice taking its place, the onomatopoeic *s*'s over-ride the fragility of the imagined voice, and the triple metres, especially in line twelve, collapse into faltering prose: 'Heard no more again far or near.' By the fourth stanza, all exuberance is gone, the metres become ordinary trochees (the dactyls return briefly in line fifteen, but again the wind's hissing *th*'s erase them), and all the rhymes are doubled, feminine, and pathetic. In this poem, which begins *in media res*, with the vivid, convincing projection of the inner world upon the outer, the real wind works against the calling voice, dissolving it utterly. There is none of 'Under the Waterfall's congruence of the twain.

The 'labouring man' who speaks in 'In the British Museum' (315) stares at the base of an old, blank marble pillar and looks 'not quite as if [he] saw, / But as if [he] heard'. Though empty, the stone is simply eloquent, rhyming the facts of its age and origins with the observer's imaginative recreation of those facts:

—'I know no art, and I only view
A stone from a wall,
But I am thinking that stone has echoed
The voice of Paul;

'Paul as he stood and preached beside it
Facing the crowd,
A small gaunt figure with wasted features,
Calling out loud

'Words that in all their intimate accents
          Pattered upon
That marble front, and were wide reflected,
          And then were gone.

'I'm a labouring man, and know but little,
          Or nothing at all;
But I can't help thinking that stone once echoed
          The voice of Paul.'

                                    (Stanzas IV–VII)

This eloquent, creative dreaming invests the inanimate with meaning, 'intimate accents', and informs human reverie. In 'In A Museum' (358), Hardy thinks:

Such a dream is Time that the coo of this ancient bird
Has perished not, but is blent, or will be blending
Mid visionless wilds of space with the voice that I heard,
In the full-fugued song of the universe unending.

                                    (Stanza II)

Similarly, in 'At a House in Hampstead: Sometime the Dwelling of John Keats' (530), the poet muses:

Pleasanter now it is to hold
That here, where sang he, more of him
Remains than where he, tuneless, cold,
          Passed to the dim.

                                    (Stanza VIII)

Again and again, it is the voices, the singers, the songs that wed Now and Then, Here and There. 'Rhyme, Ballad-rhymer', and there's no forgetting.

The little epitaph-poem from *Late Lyrics and Earlier*, 'Sacred to the Memory' (633), can stand, especially in its second stanza, as a metaphor of Hardy's poetry and rhyming. His words might be 'clearly carven' in 'bare conventionality', but his

     . . . full script is not confined
To that stone space, but stands deep lined
Upon the landscape high and low.

Hardy's mastery of the techniques of his craft was, like his analogous architectural skills, hard-earned and thorough—even when

> So little cause for carolings
> Of such ecstatic sound
> Was written on terrestrial things
> Afar or nigh around.　　　(119)

His experiments, accomplishments, and triumphs with rhyme are more than usually various, the effects ranging through the bizarre, brash, humorous, plain, and predictable to the deft and exquisitely subtle. They must not be taken for granted.

NOTES

1. This closure is reminiscent of that of Dylan Thomas's 'Twenty-four Years': 'In the final direction of the elementary town / I advance for as long as forever is.'
2. One other Hardy poem, 'Yuletide in a Younger World', has a superficially similar rhyme-scheme (stanza one: ABCDBB), but, apart from the repeated A-rhyme in all four stanzas, it has not 'Proud Songsters' ' intricate rhyme-links between stanzas.
3. The concentrated AABBA, feminine rhyme-scheme gets out of hand in the last stanza:

   > Why not sempiternal
   > Thou and I? Our vernal
   > 　Brightness keeping,
   > 　Time outleaping;
   > Passed the hodiernal!

4. Tom Paulin, *Thomas Hardy: The Poetry of Perception* (1975), pp. 30, 15.
5. *The Literary Notes of Thomas Hardy*, edited by Lennart A. Björk, Volume I, (Göteborg, Sweden: Acta Universitatis Gothoburgensis, 1974), Item 869. Hardy's underlining.
6. *Literary Notes*, Item 1079. Hardy's underlining.

3

'Emotion Put into Measure': Meaning in Hardy's Poetry

by S. C. NEUMAN

'Poetry', wrote Thomas Hardy, 'is emotion put into measure. The emotion must come by nature, but the measure can be acquired by art' (*Life*, p. 300). The remark was a chagrined reproof to reviewers who thought his *Wessex Poems* a loss to fiction and no gain at all to poetry. Seeing only a philosophy of 'pessimism' in the poems, they were not about to notice, certainly not to commend, what he called his 'art of concealing art' (*Life*, p. 301) in measure. But as a poet, Hardy was unfortunate in more than the 'pessimism' which so preoccupied his reviewers. His own response to a reader asking about the autobiographical detail behind *Jude the Obscure* diverted attention from the poetry as poetry. 'Speaking generally, there is more autobiography in a hundred lines of Mr. Hardy's poetry than in all the novels', he caused the reader to be answered (*Life*, p. 392), and a biographical criticism which explicates every nuance of loss or remorse, every slightest fluctuation of sensation or spirit supposed as generative of the poems has risen to rival that of Hardy as a 'poet of ideas'. In his own lifetime, it was other poets who approached his work with the recognition of its technical skill he thought due to it. A book of holograph poems by 'some forty or fifty living poets' presented to him shortly after his seventy-ninth birthday 'was almost his first awakening to the consciousness than an opinion had silently grown up . . . that he was no mean power in the contemporary world of poetry' (*Life*, pp. 389–90). The poet/critics, John Crowe Ransom, Yvor Winters, Donald Davie: after his death, these first gave Hardy the serious consideration as craftsman which his definition of poetry demanded.

They gave it with frequently remarked reservations about the emotion: Hardy relies on anecdote with possibilities for the sentimental which he does not always refrain from over-exploiting; if his diction is sometimes forceful and startlingly effective, it is also sometimes forced and gratingly archaic. Nor is many a reader initially any more convinced by the poet's 'measure' than by his 'emotion'. Random reading in the nine-hundred-odd poems turns up a disquieting number of lines little better than, say, ' "What is it, Ike?" inquired his wife' (668). The colloquial diction and nickname of the question contradicting, to no apparent poetic end, the formally regular metre, the forcing of that metre upon our attention by the pedantic *inquired* and by the long *i*'s of three of its stressed syllables: this prosody will not convert us to Hardy's ballads. 'Clack, clack, clack, went the mill-wheel as I came' and the rhyme in the same poem of 'clacking' with 'quacking' (880) make us regret some of the possibilities of onomatopoeia while the domesticated trochees of 'I was sitting / She was knitting' (365) are as risible as the gallant's cynical 'Is it so? / Ha-ha! Ho!' (883).

The case against Hardy's poetry on just such gleanings as these is a familiar and partly justifiable one. Yet few of us abandon his poetry; we return, despite our reservations, again and again; we become converted by degrees. The poems convince us not because we are 'pessimists', not because we interest ourselves in Hardy's transformation of guilt-ridden grief at his wife's death into superb poetry, not even because we are moved by his gift for seeing the passing moment as charged with significance. We are convinced by their art. When Hardy defined poetry as 'emotion put into measure', he was not telling us yet again that sound must echo sense. He was asserting, as Edith Sitwell would after him, that rhythm is 'to the world of sound, what light is to the world of sight. It shapes and gives new meaning'.[1] He was recognizing, as Valéry—that most lucid of all the Modernists—had recognized, that prosody is in itself a language, arbitrary certainly, but no more arbitrary than syntax or vocabulary,[2] that, like language, it conveys, in its own right, a 'rational content' (*Life*, p. 301). He was insisting that we take his definition literally, that we treat 'measure', not as *echoing* sense, but as *having* sense. That insistence contributes much to Hardy's distinctive voice and makes many a poem whose archaic diction, inverted syntax or sentimental anecdote we have initially scorned rewarding. Take the dialogue between 'The Master and the Leaves'. I reproduce it with Hardy's manuscript revisions.[3]

I

We are budding, Master, budding,
   We of your favourite tree;
March drought and April flooding
   Arouse us merrily,
Our stemlets [newly] studding;   [*brightly*]
   And yet you do not see!

II

We are fully woven for summer
   In stuff of limpest green,
The twitterer and the hummer
   Here rest [of nights, unseen,]   [*their rounds between*]
While like a long-roll drummer
   The nightjar thrills the treen.

III

We are turning yellow, Master,
   And next we are turning red,
And faster then and faster
   Shall seek our rooty bed,
All wasted in disaster!
   [But you lift not your head.]   [*The magic show we spread!*]

IV

—I mark your early going,
   And that you'll soon be clay,
I have seen your summer showing
   As in my youthful day;
But why I seem unknowing
   Is too [sunk in] to say.   [*deep down*]

As with so many of Hardy's verses, the first stanza of this one
promises less than the poet delivers; we are apt to resist the effect
of its caesurae, of the repetition of the first line and of the
recurrent closed *d* of the stanza: these leaves seem to be popping
out rather than budding. Moreover, this exuberant effect seems
contradicted by

March / drought and / April / flooding /

where the two initial stresses and the diphthongal / a / retard
the line's movement in a manner at odds with both the sense and

the sound of *merrily*. The rhyme of the secondary stress of
merrily on the masculine *tree/see* demonstrates one of Hardy's
favourite effects but initially it frustrates the prosodic expectations
set up by the poem's strong rhythms and introduces a faltering
step. 'Stemlets newly studding' may well strike us as precious;
its *st-ts-st-d* variation certainly hammers the redundant fecundity
of these leaves home, the more so since Hardy's revision of
brightly to *newly* brings the adjective's vowel into affinity with
that of *studding* and the consequent combination of alliteration
and near-assonance insists upon the repetitive *budding* of the
stanza's first line.

Yet, as we read on, we realize that some of what seem to be
the infelicitous effects of this stanza's prosody convey much of
the poem's emotion. In a stanza which opens with a hypermetrical
line for lightness, which substitutes two iambs in the second line
to introduce a rising rhythm and which uses short vowels and
four feminine rhymes to send the reader tripping through spring,
the spondaic *March drought* hints that all is not so frolicsome as
these leaves would have us believe. The diphthong of *drought*,
repeated in *arouse*, is balanced by the long, tense vowel, unusual
in the stanza, of its only masculine rhyme, *tree/see*. That rhyme
sets up the contrast between nature and man, and renders subtle
the rhyme on *merrily* which must remain secondary to the
dialogue between leaves and master. By defeating our expectations, that rhyme also undercuts the word's sense; Hardy uses
the poem's prosody in a manner contradictory to its semantic
and imagistic content in order to intimate a darker emotion
behind this cheerful spring.

He makes that suggestion stronger in the stanza's last line,
a line perfectly regular, but monosyllabically so. Where he
has used alliteration and assonance throughout the stanza to
further stress stressed syllables, in this line the alliteration of *yet
you* and the assonance of *you do* make the value of the unstressed
syllables approach that of the stressed and so lend the line
weightiness and inertia. The modulation of the short $/\wedge/$
(budding), which has been the stanza's dominant vowel, to the
longer, darker $/ u /$, the line's stark simplicity and weighty
slowness as compared to what has gone before, its culminating
long $/ i /$: all intimate a human grief greatly at odds with nature's
ebullience. That is, the poem has a subject which forms no part

of its lexical and syntactic surface: the unspoken grief of the master.

The second stanza does not allude to the indifferent master but is given·over to summer's limpid fullness. On the poem's surface, the twitterers and hummers and the nightjars figure with equal favour, equal emphasis, equal harmony: two lines for each with interlocking rhymes across the pairs. But the discordant emotion prosodically suggested in the first stanza Hardy reintroduces here in a metrical contrast between day and night. The twitterer and the hummer belong to the day: their polysyllabic, hypermetrical lines, their short vowels, are onomatopoeic for the lightness—and inconsequence—of their song. Hardy marks the transition to night by noting that the birds are now 'unseen'. The negative, its isolation by caesurae, and its rhyming position again indicate the care with which Hardy revised. Not only is the cancelled variant of the line syntactically inverted and semantically imprecise, but the revision lets *unseen* resonate against 'you do not see' in Stanza I and so keeps the master's indifference as an aural motif. As Hardy marks the transition to night, the stressed vowels lengthen (*night, unseen*), metre becomes more regular, and the strong caesura before *unseen* introduces the first drum-roll:

> The / twitterer / and the / hummer /
> Here rest / of nights, / unseen, /
> While like / a long- / roll / drummer, /
> The night / jar thrills / the treen. /

The newly introduced diphthongs and long vowels, the sudden preponderance of monosyllables, the variation on *night*, the extra stress which springs the rhythm at the nightjar's 'long-roll', the modulation on the closed *d* to *t* to *th* to *t* across the constant interplay of liquids and sonorants in the bird's song: these variations are carefully calculated to counterpoint the general metrical regularity and so to make the nightjar's song less cheerfully innocuous than that of the unnamed birds of day. When we hear that, with the introduction of night, we have returned to a predominantly iambic pattern, we realize that the master of 'And yet you do not see' has been aurally with us the while.

His metrical and stanzaic rhythms well established, Hardy uses them, in a way which typifies his prosody, to suggest the poem's *unstated* grief. The surviving manuscript of 'The Master and the Leaves' shows that he originally intended that the surface of Stanza III, like that of II, should be given entirely to the leaves' self-description. Like the first stanza, this one is heavily onomatopoeic, relying for speed on repetition and on anacrusis in the feminine-rhymed lines. But here the rapid metre suggests not the ebullience of spring but a new urgency. Hardy intimates the cyclic reasons for that urgency by carefully varying the repetitive patterns of Stanza I. The 'We are . . .' phrase which has opened the description of each of the seasons is, as it was in I, interrupted by a direct address to the master. But the phrase is this time repeated in its entirety ('we are turning red'), emphasizing the finality connoted by its lexical content and, more importantly, moving the vocative address to the end of the line where it receives extreme emphasis. The variation shifts the poem's focus from leaves to master and it is this shift, as much as autumn's promise of severer frosts to come, that creates the stanza's ominous undertone.

The whole stanza is precisely balanced, two lines for each assertion, each involving an onomatopoeic repetition, about the fast-falling leaves. Nothing simpler, more logical, or duller than to make the last two lines a similarly contained thought as indeed Hardy had done in the manuscript version with its banal cancelled line. But the revision lets the last two lines imply the poem's powerful emotion: line 5 sums up the description of the autumn leaves, 'all wasted in disaster'; line 6, simply because the stanzaic rhythm has been that of two lines per assertion, the assertions linked by rhyme, implies, by turning to the master, that he too is 'wasted in disaster'. Coming after the urgent rhythm of the rest of the stanza and carrying us back to the vocative address at the end of its first line, this line is emphatically final. It stands in relation to its stanza as did the last line of Stanza I and is so nearly parallel to it as to act like a refrain. In the variation on the 'refrain', however, we see how much closer we have come to the poem's tragic emotion:

> And yet / you do / not see! /
> But you / lift not / your head. /

The stress pattern of the two lines is identical but the slightest change in syntax alters all. The stress on *yet* remains ambiguous, introducing contrast with the leaves, but also, in its temporal denotation, suggesting that the master may yet respond to the leaves' beauty at some future time. The parallel *but* holds out no such hope, nor does the shift in stress. By varying the pattern to stress *not* rather than *do*, Hardy has emphasized regret rather than hope. By stressing *you* rather than *yet*, he makes the lines faintly accusatory; they seem to demand an explanation, facilitating the dialogue's transition from leaves to master.

The rigid stanzaic pattern of 'The Master and the Leaves' has established its own rhythm of the four seasons; that *rhythm*, not any direct statement, equates the master's words with winter. At the same time, the prosodic characteristics associated with the master throughout the poem alter the established pattern for the opening lines of the stanza. The repetitions and caesurae which gave such urgent motion to Stanzas I and III are here replaced by a colloquial, but grave, speech. The monosyllabic, stressed *mark* substitutes an iamb for the anacrusis we have had opening previous stanzas; its andante is a contrapuntal response to the allegro of each of the preceding 'We are . . .' openings. Not only does the master's speech lack all the hectic effects of the leaves' stanzas, but, as he refuses to explain his indifference, the lengthening vowels and monosyllables of the last two lines weight the poem with melancholy. The only extant revision to the stanza suggests once again how careful and subtle were many of Hardy's prosodic emendations. *Deep down*, with its alliteration, long vowels and nasal ending has become a convention to suggest the weight of grief; Hardy himself used *down* most movingly to this end in two of the 'refrain' lines of 'During Wind and Rain'. But his revision in 'The Master and the Leaves' to *sunk in* lets him repeat the back vowel and the nasal of *seem unknowing*; this repetition and the stress on a short vowel (*sunk*) create an enervating rather than a raging or wildly despairing grief. As *sunk in* repeats and condenses the sounds of *seem unknowing*, the two phrases aurally re-create both the solipsism which is the result of that grief and its anaesthetizing effect.

If I have belaboured the analysis, it is because it serves to make an essential point about the *meaning*, the 'rational content' of Hardy's prosody. A reader of 'The Master and the Leaves' will immediately recognize that the poem's subject is not the ostensible dialogue but grief. That recognized, the leaves' fate becomes symbolic and two images in the poem imply the reason for the suffering. We can read *clay* as metonymical for *death*. So too the *long-roll* of the nightjar: the drumbeat used at funerals and at executions, the long-roll functions ambiguously to suggest bereavement as the cause of the master's grief and perhaps to imply that the grief will also be his executioner. But while its tropes may imply a *reason* for grief, nowhere does the poem *articulate* grief. Its entire point is *unarticulated* emotion: ' "why I seem unknowing / Is too sunk in to say!" '. But one of poetry's functions *is* to articulate emotion. This poem does so in the rhythmical ways I have noted and by pivoting on the strongly emphasized *unseen*. Throughout the first stanza and the first lines of the second, the dominant vowels have been / $\wedge$ / and / i /. Both culminate in *unseen* / $\wedge$nsin / to disappear until the *seem-sunk* sequence at the end of the poem. The grief behind this poem may go unspoken, *unseen*, but as the entire sound pattern of the poem shifts with the emphasis on the very word which, both in its literal sense and in its metaphorical sense of *not understood*, forms a large part of the insistence on unarticulated emotion, as assonances, rhymes and metrical variations counterpoint and undercut the leaves' ebullience, as the stanzaic rhythm forces us to displace our expectation of winter on to the master's speech, grief does not go unheard. In such superbly calculated lacunae between what is said, and what is heard, Hardy finds his subject again and again.

Hardy's self-conscious use of prosodic effects is at its most overt in his humorous and broadly ironic poems. In 'Liddell and Scott', scholarly concerns recede before the comic haste of triple rhymes on the names of scholars and their disciplines, on abbreviations and on Greek letters and words. In such verse, Hardy fashions his rhyme to achieve the maximum incongruity, cancelling, for example, an amusing but not startling rhyme on *conceivings / believings* for the punning rhyme on *Donnegan / con again*. The whole enterprise of dictionary making is undercut by a rhyme scheme and a dimeter / tetrameter arrangement that gallops through the dictionary so quickly that the lexicographers' decision to abandon work for dinner and the final rhyme on *fiddle / Liddell* are an outrageous but also an appropriate conclusion.

The *tour de force* of 'Liddell and Scott', so largely dependent on comic incongruity of rhyme, is more than equalled by the less well-known 'A Refusal'. There the Dean's considered, indeed pedantic, arguments for the principles upon which dead poets are to be buried in Westminster is parodied by the orotund enjambement of up to six consecutive lines at a time; those same considered arguments are comically contradicted by the emotional haste of the dimeter. The rhyme either puns—as does the opening identical rhyme on *Westminster / minster*, following hard on the description of the Dean as *grave*—or sets up incongruous contrasts. When the Dean rhymes *Christian* with *Philistian*, the eye rhyme suggests that perhaps the disputed poets represent *proportion* where he represents *distortion*. The rhymed contrasts gain ambiguity until we place the Dean opposite his enunciated position. As each succeeding candidate to the Poet's Corner is named, the extent of the Dean's Philistine outrage is conveyed by more and more improbable rhymes: *environ / Byron*; then, for Shelley, *tablet / gablet*; and finally, for the culminating desecration, *skin burn / chin burn / Swinburne*.

Such overtly comic prosody has limited uses but the self-conscious play it reveals shows up in poem after poem of Hardy's. A troubadour youth rambles

> With Life for lyre,
> The beats of being raging
> In me like fire.   (166)

In a poem more given to the dismal resonances of lines like 'Untombed although' than to alliteration, its use in these lines identifies the thumping of the troubadour's heartbeat with the thrumming of the Muses' lyre. Not one of Hardy's most successful metrical pleasantries. But the play *is* successful in the poem's final stanza—

> ... though whiling
> The time somehow
> In walking, talking, smiling,
> I live not now—

where the third line, metronomic in its regularity, parallelism and internal rhyme, literally marks 'time' for the living dead man.

Sometimes Hardy uses puns to call attention to his own cleverness in devising forms. 'Regret Not Me' achieves its cavalier effect through tercets which build up momentum by adding a foot per line: each stanza begins with a dimeter line, expands into a trimeter, and ends with a tetrameter which, in all but one instance, is divided into dimeters by a medial caesura, so circling back on the first line to encapsulate the stanza. The effect is as elaborately self-conscious as is the narrator's self-effacing disclaimer: 'Regret not me.' But far from taking this contrived pattern seriously, Hardy puns on it in a trimeter line in which he hypothesizes 'Some triple-timed romance'. He then draws our attention to both this alliteration and to the coupling of dimeters in the tetrameter line following:

> And lightly dance
> Some triple-timed romance
> In coupled figures, and forget mischance.

Hardy does not specify the identity of either the narrator or those left behind, but the puns suggest that the speaker's carefree attitude as he contemplates those who forget him by coupling anew is as artificial as is his verse form. By drawing attention to the artifice of the form, the poet has also drawn attention to the artifice of the emotion its surface expresses and has pointed the reader to the poem's underlying emotion: an ironic bitterness that the dead are so quickly forgotten.

At other times Hardy will draw attention to his form as a way of heightening his readers' visual imagination. 'The Fallow Deer at the Lonely House' is clear about its architectonics from its first line:

> One / without / looks in / to-night / (551).

The stresses on the contrasting prepositions metrically give the rationale behind the poem's two stanzas: the first presents the deer *outside*, looking in; the second gives us the people *inside* and what they *do not see*. Hardy's problem is to make his readers more perceptive than the people in the poem. He must describe what 'We do not discern' and do it so that it truly registers if the contrast between those looking and those not seeing is to be effective. He does this by altering the stress pattern in his concluding couplet:

> We do not discern those eyes
> Wondering, aglow,
> Fourfooted, tiptoe.

The poem is irreparably flawed by the syntax of these lines, but their prosody to some extent overrides that syntax to create a visual image of what the poem represents as unseen. While the substitution of 'Wondering, aglow' carries all the sense of encapsulating closure which Hardy usually makes his couplets bear, the last line's secondary stresses and alliteration are so strong they make possible a rhetorical reading of the line as 'four-footed'. The metrical pun makes the four-footed deer concrete; it forces into the forefront of the reader's visual imagination that which has gone unseen by the 'we' of the poem.

Beginning with the preface to *Wessex Poems*, Hardy insisted that his poetry was 'in a large degree dramatic or personative in conception' (*Collected Poems*, p. 6). Some of its most distinctive effects, both brash and subtle, result from the interplay of colloquial speech rhythms with more formally regular metrical and stanzaic patterns. 'The Ruined Maid' is an ironic instance. Its stanzaic rhythm is the rhetorical one of question or exclamation and understated explanation. That rhetoric creates the rhythmical alternation of envious amazement and worldly self-satisfaction. The poem's success depends on precisely those effects most apt to make us wince until we are far enough along to understand its rhetoric. The falsely stressed rhyme on the last syllable of *prosperi-ty, compa-ny, la-dy, melancho-ly*, registers as a parody of rigid adherence to ballad metre's regularity and so characterizes the 'raw country girl'. For not only does the ballad form bring with it connotations of rural ingenuousness appropriate to her, but the stress its regularity places on *prosperi-ty*, the inverted *bright feathers three*, and *high compa-ny* makes audible the girl's longing. The repetition, whether of whole words or by alliteration or assonance, only intensifies that longing.

The country girl's dialect and accents of envy stand contrapuntally against the correct and laconic responses of the ruined maid. Hardy revised carefully to achieve the off-handedly col-

loquial but still correct colour of her speech: ' "That's the
advantage of ruin" '⁴ became the more sardonic ' "One's pretty
lively when ruined" ' and the drawn-out regret of ' "Ah—no!" '
was cancelled for the condescending accents of ' "My dear" ', the
phrase contrasting sharply with its use in her friend's initial
onrush of admiration—' "O 'Melia, my dear, this does everything
crown!" ' The complacency which marks 'Melia's speech, as
well as its sardonic quality, depends on the absence of the
repetitiveness that characterizes her country friend. Nowhere is
the difference between the speech of the two so evident as in
their use of caesurae. The country girl pauses to exclaim, to pile
up evidence of amazement by repetition, parallelism and conjunction. 'Melia's initial assenting caesurae have an air of finality
(' "Yes: that's how we dress …" '; ' "True. One's pretty lively
…" ') while the medial caesura of her last line sums up all the
irony of her luxurious life: ' "a raw country girl, such as you be,
/ Cannot quite expect that. You ain't ruined," said she'.

The poem inverts those Victorian moral tales which point out
that luxury bought by sin brings with it bitter shame. Harvey
Gross suggests that the ruined maid's 'pride … is qualified by
certain misgivings'⁵ and perhaps her lapse into dialect in the last
line supports the interpretation. The modified ballad form, the
couplet rhymes, the ironic variations on the ballad refrain: all
these, however, keep the poem lighthearted and leave serious
moral judgements a comfortable distance from the lady's bright
feathers. But there is no delight in escaping a parable's moral
unless the escape is a narrow one. This poem's moral *is* present,
predictably, in the prosody. I have been speaking of the poem as
a modified ballad: the decasyllabic lines often expand to eleven
or even twelve syllables and, if their anapests create the rush of
the country girl's amazed wonder and keep the verse light, the
missing moral implication nonetheless enters by the modification
of the ballad stanza into hymnal long measure. The metrical
allusion provides the moral seriousness and makes the moral
judgement which go unstated in the poem. It also makes the
poem more sardonic than could any mere words exchanged
between 'Melia and her country acquaintance.

Some of Hardy's most haunting effects he achieved in an
opposite fashion, by abandoning colloquial speech in favour of
nonce song forms which he used with telling substitutions and

enjambements. Up to four lines in each stanza of 'How She Went
to Ireland' (906) are refrain-like variations on each other:

> Dora's gone to Ireland
>   Through the sleet and snow;
> Promptly she has gone there
>   In a ship, although
> Why she's gone to Ireland
>   Dora does not know.
>
> That was where, yea, Ireland,
>   Dora wished to be:
> When she felt, in lone times,
>   Shoots of misery,
> Often there, in Ireland,
>   Dora wished to be.
>
> Hence she's gone to Ireland,
>   Since she meant to go,
> Through the drift and darkness
>   Onward labouring, though
> That she's gone to Ireland
>   Dora does not know.

Death is never mentioned but the entire rhythm of the poem is
one of closure, finality. Not only is Dora's going from the 'here'
of the poem a constantly varied refrain, but the powerful posi-
tioning of *Ireland* in two lines of each stanza and the opening of
five lines of the poem with the strong trochaic *Dora* always turn
the poem back on its initial statement. Other parallelisms have
similar rhythmic effects. 'Sleet and snow' are rhythmically reiterated in the even more suggestive 'drift and darkness' of the
last stanza; again, the poem's self-enclosure leaves only the
irreducible fact of Dora's leaving which becomes strongly elegaic
in its obsessiveness. That the tragedy of Dora's absence lies in
the manner of her going Hardy expresses metrically. The poem's
rhyme scheme is, for him, an understated one: the first and fifth
lines rhyme identically on *Ireland*, the third has no rhyme. The
perfectly regular trimeter of these three lines lets the verses lilt.
The remaining three lines rise by virtue of masculine rhyme but
the melancholy lost by the sacrifice of the falling rhythm is more
than compensated for by the strongly elegaic rhymes in the first

and last stanzas on long *o*. The most suggestive prosodic effect, however, is the enjambement of the concessive *although* of Stanza I and *though* of III, against the clauses following. The lines can be scanned as catalectic trochaic but the caesura in effect acts as a weak syllable and so substitutes an iamb in the terminal foot.

> In a / ship, / although /
> Onward / labouring/, though /

The use of the disyllabic *labouring* and the reduction of *although* to *though* in the second instance shift the pause from the end of the trochaic foot to the beginning of the iambic. The variation is just sufficient to maintain our interest while the caesura, the metrical shift and the emphatic terminal position of *although / though* imbue Dora's leaving with an ominousness missing from the simple statement 'Dora's gone to Ireland'. The enjambement against the noun clauses, themselves emphasized by an inversion which places them at the head of the clauses for which they serve as direct objects, draws to the foreground the unstated reason for her going and the irrevocable finality of her having gone. Seldom in English poetry has the conjunctive adverb, simply by virtue of its position in the line, been made to bear so much meaning.

This use of various combinations of caesurae, substitution, enjambement and syntactic inversion to make one word bear meaning far in excess of or even contradictory to its lexical function, or to make it the emotional crux of an anecdote which is often only sketched in, is a good part of what we recognize as Hardy's 'voice'. In a poem like 'The Destined Pair', the nonce stanza, consisting of an *abab* quatrain and an indented tercet, seems to promise little but fractured form, but the enjambement of quatrain and tercet in facts unifies the form by effecting, in each stanza, the transition from the man and woman as separate and ignorant of one another to the man and woman as couple. The technique's success becomes marked in the last stanza:

> Would Fate have been kinder
> To keep night between them?—
> Had he failed to find her
> And time never seen them
>   Unite; so that, caught
>   In no burning love-thought,
>   She had faded unsought?

Here the enjambement of quatrain and tercet makes the entire poem pivot on *unite*, the verb which is the culmination of the figures' approach to one another described in the first two stanzas and which makes the last stanza's question an hypothetical one. That question implies tragedy or at least unhappiness as the consequence of the figures' coming together; the enjambement which moves *unite* to the strong initial position in the tercet, turning the poem on the verb, ironically suggests that the union itself is the tragedy. The line's metrical variation reinforces the suggestion. Hardy has adhered to an hypermetrical dimeter throughout the rest of the poem. The *unite* line is its only trimeter and is slowed even further by its two caesurae. Once again, one of the pauses acts as the unstressed value in an iamb, counterpointing this line against the rapid anapests of the rest of the poem:

Unite; / so that/, caught /

The enjambement of *this* line with

In no burn / ing love-thought, /

which, while it scans to match its anapestic counterparts in the first two stanzas, also resists the meter by its unusually strong secondary stresses, makes these two lines the poem's metrical pivot. The enjambement and variation isolate *caught* and balance it against *unite* to extend the poem's meaning beyond that inherent in the sketchy anecdote and to imply the reason for the poem's question. Prosodic variation tells us that the union itself has been the cause of the tragedy, that union has meant the woman's entrapment.

When we acknowledge Hardy's claim that he is using 'artistic form' to convey a 'rational content' and recognize that that 'content' is one which the lexical and even symbolic values of the poems often leave unstated or only indirectly stated, a surprising number of the *Collected Poems* gain in richness. So too the evocativeness of those poems most frequently treated as Hardy's 'best' becomes more explicable. 'Overlooking the River Stour', for example, is typically structured: three stanzas visualize an arrested moment, a fourth ironically points out that the true significance of the moment went unperceived. But the piece owes its elegaic irony to far more than this structure and the cue provided by the last stanza's 'alack'. An unease, produced by metrical variation, pervades the poem. Four metrically regular refrain lines per stanza, varying line lengths and predominant iambs and anapests suggest the recurrent rhythms of the swallows' swooping flight.[6] Acting contrapuntally against this rhythm are stopped c's and, beginning in the third stanza, stopped d's, sounds evocative of stasis and closure rather than of flight. The third lines of all but the second stanza also counterpoint the birds' flight, this time using Hardy's tendency to substitute rhetorical stress for metrical accent; the lines can be scanned regularly but only by considerably subordinating the strong secondary stresses:

> In the wet June's last beam:
>
> Through the day's morning sheen
>
> Through the pane's drop-drenched glaze.

Particularly in the last instance, where alliteration reinforces the secondary stresses and where *drop-drenched* recalls the previous stanza's *dripped*, it is difficult not to read the line as ending in something very close to two spondees. Its movement is deliberate and weighty, extending the force of the poem's shift in imagery from 'stream-shine' to rain. The co-operation of image and metre to greatly intensify the regret named in the last stanza culminates in that stanza's violation of the established regularity of the refrain:

> And never I turned my head, alack,
>
>   While these things met my gaze
>
> Through the pane's drop-drenched glaze,
>
> To see the more behind my back . . . .
>
> O never I turned, but let, alack,
>
>   These less things hold my gaze!

The entire modulation is that familiar to us from lesser poems. The refrain's first line, with its conventional calling up of regret, when it is repeated, introduces caesurae and the contradictory *but* to dwell on loss. Its second line, repeated, strengthens the evocation of loss and regret by modifying the stress pattern with the introduction of an adjective; the stress now shifts to *less* and compares the described landscape of the poem—*these less things*—with what is *not* described—*the more behind my back*. The shift in stress, the pauses, the use of the comparative *more* (with its dolorous / ɔr /) as substantive: all use form to pull the attention away from the flight of the swallows, to articulate as emotionally significant what the poem's speaker cannot describe because he did not perceive it.

The same contrapuntal organization of sound to present what is unseen or unheard by the poem's speaker explains Hardy's use of 'wan wistlessness' in 'The Voice', a use which even the poem's greatest admirers have found difficult to accept.[7] One of Hardy's finest onomatopoeic effects is surely this poem's rhyme on *call to me / all to me*; the dactyls' falling rhythms, by capturing the woman's receding voice, are deeply evocative of the distance separating the speaker from her. The *listlessness / wistlessness* rhyme gave Hardy more difficulty for it records the speaker doubting even the sound of the woman's voice. Hardy's manuscript describes her as 'ever consigned to existlessness'.[8] That abstraction he replaces with 'dissolved to wan wistlessness' which has its own syntactic problem: we can reconstruct what he intends by *wistless* and apply it to the shade and we rather expect her to be *wan*; we find it more difficult to determine the poet's meaning when one attribute describes the other rather than the shade. The aural effect of the revised rhyme, however, very accurately evokes the speaker's sensation. As the shade's imagined presence momentarily yields to the reality of the wind, the dactyls which gave it voice are heard again, but they are heard as voiceless consonants, as sibilants; the woman's call is reduced to a whisper, 'Heard no more'. Only a reduced aural memory of the voice remains in the last fractured stanza so often remarked as one of Hardy's most notable successes in the use of organic form. The speaker is left *faltering* amid *falling* leaves, and the imagined *calling*. The echoic effect of the dactyl has given way to the grief of the abbreviated falling trochee. The ghost, like that of 'After a Journey', which echoes 'A Voice' in its rhyme on *draw me / awe me*, has become 'voiceless' (289).

Many of these poems pivot on the question 'What difference, then?' (279). A prosodic turn like that of 'The Voice' defines the different emotional significance of 'Beeny Cliff' when its horsewoman is no longer there. The poem is a study in balance. The initial harmony of reciprocated emotion is aurally as well as lexically present in the parallelism of 'loved so' and 'loved me':

The wo / man whom / I loved / so, / and who / loyally / loved me.

The stresses balance and encapsulate the parallelism; the pattern is reiterated in the alliterations and assonances which describe the actual scene: 'pale mews plained', 'waves seemed far away / . . . engrossed in saying their ceaseless babbling say'. The aural balance is momentarily and ominously destroyed as the susurrus of the waves gives way to the closed sounds and heavy stresses of a *clear-sunned March day* which approaches the spondaic. But in the final line of Stanza III, with its medial caesura and internal rhyme, balance is aurally as well as imagistically restored. The final emotional wrench comes in another parallel structure. Again, the poem's grief goes largely unstated. The woman is 'elsewhere'; the euphemism and the hiatus Paulin has noted as being like a 'catch in the voice'[9] imply too great a grief to be openly acknowledged on the poem's lexical surface. But 'that wandering western sea' of the poem's opening line, its waves breaking in voiceless iambs, has become 'that wild weird western shore', in the last stanza's variation. The *w*'s, closed *d*'s and long vowels of *wild weird* make a reading of the phrase as trochaic an arbitrary assimilation into the predominant metre of the line; in fact, the two words must be equally emphasized, giving us three pounding and grief-stricken stresses in a row before the gentle sibilancy of *western sea* also gives way to the dolorous and thrice-repeated / ɔr / of the rhyme on *shore*. Hardy has contrived once again to make a grief 'too sunk in to say' heard.

Hardy preserved his note 'that a clever thrush, and a stupid nightingale, sing very much alike' (*Life*, p. 252). Art alone does not enable the thrush to compensate for an inferior voice; the nightingale's superior gifts will not find their highest expression without art. The sardonic diary entry is but another statement of the balance in these poems which we respond to as distinctively Hardyean. We experience many of them as emotionally reticent; their language is often imprecise or painfully awkward about their emotion or they are laconic about the details of the anecdote or situation which substantiates that emotion. Yet the poems overwhelm us by the emotion implicit in their rhythms. Before that, we feel ourselves before the heart exposed. That balance is a large part of their art: their deliberate reticence saves most of them from the dangers of sentimentality or bathos; the emotion which does make itself *heard* infuses the individual case or the passing moment of the anecdote with significance. Out of the contrapuntal play between the poems' two languages, between prosody and lexical content, Hardy shaped the meaning of many of his poems.

NOTES

1. Edith Sitwell, *Collected Poems* (1965), p. xv.
2. Paul Valéry, *Oeuvres*, ed. Jean Hytier (Paris, 1957), I, 478.
3. Italicized passages in the right-hand margin have been cancelled in the ms. copy of *Late Lyrics and Earlier* in the Dorset County Museum in favour of the bracketed passages in the final version of the poem.
4. Cancelled passages are those in the ms. of *Poems of the Past and the Present* in The Bodleian Library, Oxford.
5. Harvey Gross, *Sound and Form in Modern Poetry: A Study of Prosody from Thomas Hardy to Robert Lowell* (Ann Arbor, 1964), p. 44.
6. Tom Paulin, *Thomas Hardy: The Poetry of Perception* (1975), p. 170, notes the contribution the modified triolet rhyme makes to the effect.
7. E.g., F. R. Leavis, *New Bearings in English Poetry* (1976), p. 49.
8. Ms. of *Satires of Circumstances Lyrics and Reveries* is in the Dorset County Museum.
9. Paulin, p. 74.

4

The Mellstock Quire and Tess in Hardy's Poetry

by ROSEMARY L. EAKINS

> Probably few literary critics discern the solidarity of all the arts. Curiously enough Hardy himself dwelt upon it in a poem that seems to have been little understood, though the subject is of such interest.
>
> (*Life*, p. 300)

Hardy wrote this poem, 'Rome, The Vatican: Sala delle Muse' (70), in 1887. In it he described his regret at the inconstancy of his worship, divided between 'Form' and 'Tune', between 'Story, and Dance, and Hymn', and his reassuring revelation that these are after all only 'phases of one' Muse. It was a revelation useful or even necessary to an established novelist who was shortly to seek the attention of the public for his poetry. To find it reflected in a relationship between his poems and his novels is no more than what we should expect. A number of poems carry a title or an epigraph drawing attention to one of the novels, and the number of poems related to novels or to short stories is far larger. Even a generation before the question of the possible relationships between prose and poetry began to be earnestly and exhaustively canvassed by writers like Joyce, Hardy had woven a whole intricate web of such relationships, peculiar to his own art.

Two groups of poems stand out remarkably from the others with prose connections. The first features the Mellstock Quire (not a choir but a string band) which plays an important role in *Under the Greenwood Tree* (1872), but which is depicted rather differently in the poems. The second re-examines aspects of the character and story of *Tess of the d'Urbervilles* (1891). Together these two groups will enable us to raise most of the questions of interest about the relationships of Hardy's prose and his poems.

Under the Greenwood Tree was the work of a young man

beginning to learn what subjects could be congenial to his readers
without being uncongenial to himself. *The Poor Man and the
Lady*, which voiced a challenge to the existing order of social
classes, had failed to find a publisher; *Desperate Remedies*, a
novel of tortuous psychological analysis, had failed to sell. *Under
the Greenwood Tree* began as a project for salvaging some rural
scenes from *The Poor Man and the Lady*, which John Morley
had liked. Its title, altered from *The Mellstock Quire*, as Hardy
says in his throwaway style, 'because titles from poetry were in
fashion just then' (*Life*, p. 86), comes from a song in *As You Like
It*, and sets its scene not only in Hardy's native Dorset but also
in an idealized pastoral Arden—the country as seen by town-
dwellers. The novel's naïve young 'ordinary' lovers and its naïve,
comic countrymen proved more popular than anything Hardy
had written so far.

'The realities out of which [*Under the Greenwood Tree*] was
spun were material for another kind of study of this little group
of church musicians than is found in the chapters here penned
so lightly, even so farcically and flippantly at times', Hardy
wrote.[1] In the *Life* he modified this remark: 'He was accustomed
to say that . . . he had rather burlesqued them, the story not so
adequately reflecting as he could have wished in later years the
poetry and romance of their time-honoured observance' (*Life*,
p. 12). In fact the novel presents old William Dewy seriously in
the main, allowing his 'frequent melancholy' and 'firm religious
faith' (I. iii); but much space is given to his more caricatured
companions, Thomas Leaf getting almost the last moments of
the book for his foolish story of the man who made a thousand
pounds. The concern of even the more intelligent quire members
is principally with 'party feeling' (I. vi) and the threat posed by
the prospect of the harmonium. In his poems Hardy could and
did refine the image projected in this early novel.

Hardy, then, wanted to make amends to the quire whose real-
life prototype included his own grandfather, father and uncle;
but this was not his only motive for using material from *Under
the Greenwood Tree* in his poems. Many poems are connected
to this novel by the fact that both make use of the same details
of place or incident from Hardy's own experience, a sharing of
matter that need make no unity of the different treatments.
'Under the Waterfall' (276), for instance, poignantly captures an

event in Hardy's own courtship which, before he wrote the poem, he had already used in both *Under the Greenwood Tree* and *Tess*. The deliberate understatement of feelings in the early novel—'It being the first time in his life that he had touched female fingers under water, Dick duly registered the sensation as rather a nice one' (though Fancy Day is shaken: II. vii)—has almost nothing in common with the depths sounded in the poem. Often, though, an apparently coincidental detail serves as signpost to important similarities of mood and theme. Thomas Voss, who bears 'the only real name' in *Under the Greenwood Tree* (*Life*, p. 92), is there left to prepare hot cider and victuals for the quire after its Christmas rounds (I. iv), but in 'Voices from Things Growing in a Churchyard' (580) is transformed into juicy, poisonous yew berries. There is no consonance between Thomas Voss's two appearances in Hardy's writing—but there is, as we shall see, a consonance in any character connected with the quire appearing in a poem of voices from the grave.

In about a dozen poems scattered through several volumes of poetry, Hardy presented a further account of the Mellstock Quire in such a way that its members gain in stature and significance. No longer even partly figures of fun, they are in these poems first and foremost men of the past. This means not only that they are dead, but that they have been a moral and spiritual force in their community in old times, according to old ways which now in a new, more secular age may appear superstitious or alien but never contemptible, and often as inaccessibly desirable as Arden itself.

The quire makes its first appearance in poetry in 'Friends Beyond' (36) (*Wessex Poems*, 1898), where local people speak from their graves in Mellstock churchyard. They include from *Under the Greenwood Tree* William Dewy and his son Reuben the Tranter or carrier, now speaking on equal terms as 'we' with the Squire and Lady Susan, using their old dialect ('Ye mid burn the old bass-viol'), yet sharing also in the more heightened, formal language which marks the collective speech of the dead. They no longer care, they say, for their old pursuits or about the activities of the living. An image used by all the dead, 'If you quire to our old tune', is given more precise significance by the Dewys' membership of the old quire, whose continuance and whose tunes they cared so strongly about in the novel. They have now achieved 'very gods' composure' and to the poet they speak as to 'fellow-wight who yet abide'. It is more significant that Hardy should give the senior Dewys—who both were, and emphatically were not, his grandfather and father or uncle—kinship with himself than with the socially superior squire and lady. Such kinship had been impossible between the narrator of a rather burlesque novel and his creatures.

Four poems concerning the quire were collected in *Time's Laughingstocks* (1909). The first two recall, in different terms, the party given by Reuben Dewy in *Under the Greenwood Tree*. Whether the first, 'The House of Hospitalities' (156), was written about the cottage which Hardy assigned to the Dewys in the novel, or that of his own family, the parties which the writer regrets were Christmas ones, with a barrel broached and 'quaint songs', 'When the folk now dead were young'.

> And the worm has bored the viol
>   That used to lead the tune,
> Rust eaten out the dial
>   That struck night's noon—

a particularly important moment when William Dewy forbade dancing until the completed striking should signify that Christmas was properly over. The speaker of the poem feels close to these 'forms of old time talking, / Who smile on me' and profoundly dissatisfied with the present, 'Now no Christmas brings in neighbours'. 'The Night of the Dance' (184) repeats details from the other poem and the novel—the viols, the spigot, the fire still receiving attention, this time from 'Old Robert' who is probably Robert Penny of the novel—and adds an accompanying cold moon and stars. This time, however, the speaker is an expectant lover looking forward, supplying a touch of added emotion as surely as a survivor looking back. He does not use dialect, but he suggests the young Dick Dewy, waiting impatiently to dance with Fancy Day and already half in love with her.

'The Rash Bride' (212), subtitled 'An Experience of the Mellstock Quire', is entirely different in structure and feeling, a narrative of the quire making its Christmas rounds at a date when its supremacy in the church was still unchallenged. The speaker, evidently not a member of the Dewy family since he calls William 'Our old bass player', not 'father' or 'grandfather', recounts the quire's active involvement in a tragic event. A young widow is revealed to have secretly acquired a new husband, jilting a young man who was hoping to please her by his singing that night. Michael (presumably Michael Mail of the novel) sternly rebukes her, she rushes away, and suddenly the whole quire finds itself taking part in a desperate search. They had come to wish her Christmas joy, they pull her dead body from the well, and Sunday next they play the Ninetieth Psalm at her burial. The speaker concludes with old William, pale and tremulous, bowing his viol, 'doomed to follow her full soon'. The quire which can pass judgement, attempt rescue, and lay to rest, has a fuller range of moral activity than that in the novel; the psalm they play at the funeral, the one which tells of time as an ever-rolling stream bearing all its sons away, suits them perfectly.

The poem which follows in *Time's Laughingstocks*, 'The Dead Quire', is equally serious. The setting is another, more recent, Christmas Eve in Mellstock. The members of the quire are dead, and their sons and grandsons keep Christmas in a new fashion, carousing at an inn as the holy day is ushered in. The reader of the novel remembers the Christmas rounds, and also William Dewy's careful guardianship of the minutes of Christmas Day. Just after midnight, 'as in old days', the voices and music of the old quire—which had aspired to 'go quietly, so as to strike up all of a sudden, like spirits' (I. iv)—miraculously sound in the ears of the young revellers, and the past chastens the present. Their voices sing (and the rhythm of the hymn echoes through the poem) '*While shepherds watch'd* ... / To, *Glory shone around.*' They act as shepherds to their descendants, conducting them, by a path followed in the novel, back to the churchyard.

This poem does look like compensation by Hardy for his 'flippant' and 'farcical' treatment of the quire in prose. After death the members of the band, no longer indifferent to earthly affairs as in 'Friends Beyond', take positive steps to correct the failings of present time, which are more serious than that noted in 'The House of Hospitalities'. Nevertheless, the poem is narrated by a 'sad man' who remains sad to the end, for the miraculous voices sang long ago and times have further changed. The sad man 'seems ... still' to sigh 'his phantasies', which suggests both that he is now dead and that the story of the dead quire was only a fantasy. We are therefore distanced from the quire by time and by more than the passing of time.

In 'Seen by the Waits' (325: *Satires of Circumstance*, 1914), the quire members are intelligent men of this world who know how to keep their own counsel. Once more making their Christmas rounds, they play outside the manor house of a lady whose husband is away. To their astonishment, they see her dancing alone in front of a mirror, and later they learn that she had just received news of the death of her 'roving spouse'. As they react with resolution to midnight suicide, they react with understanding, not outrage, to this private drama: 'Why she had danced in the gloaming / We thought, but never said.' From their vantage point in the musicians' gallery, they have watched the parisioners until they know them better than the priest does, though in the novel this knowledge was presented in more frivolous terms. Hardy continues to strengthen and deepen his account of them, bringing them close to the comprehending, compassionate poet.

'To My Father's Violin' (381: *Moments of Vision*, 1917) makes no mention of the Mellstock Quire, but lovingly evokes the Stinsford one 'Who for long years strenuously— / Son and sire— / Caught the strains' of the elder Hardy's fingering. Both 'psalm of duty' and 'trill of pleasure' are remembered by the son who sadly cons the instrument's 'present dumbness'. With 'Ten worm-wounds in your neck', 'wan / With dust-hoar', it seems as much a corpse as its master. The melancholy and respectful attitude, celebrating both enjoyment and rectitude which have passed away, is typical of the quire poems. We should perhaps group with this poem 'A Church Romance' (211) and 'One We Knew' (227), published in *Time's Laughingstocks*, about Hardy's grandmother. In the first she falls in love with her future husband while he plays in the gallery; in the second she recalls distant memories including a band playing 'The Triumph', the dance which opened the Tranter's Christmas party in *Under the Greenwood Tree*. The poem's emphasis falls on Mary Hardy and a whole range of her recollections, but the 'band gone distant' which played for both gentle and simple evokes all the same feelings of loss and regret as does the Dewys' band. 'The Triumph' is also played at 'The Dance at the Phoenix' (28) held by the King's-Own Cavalry in another poem about the strong tug of the past, although the players themselves have little importance in it. Hardy's feelings about the quire he had heard so much of could flow out into poems with other priorities, as well as gathering into a poetic statement about the quire itself. The same collection as 'To My Father's Violin' includes 'The Oxen' (403), a poem of passionate regret for the passing of old belief from the community and from the speaker himself. The 'elder' in the poem who enunciates the belief that the oxen kneel on Christmas Eve has something in common with William Dewy, who claimed to have seen it happen himself (with an angry bull). Hardy did not use this story in *Under the Greenwood Tree*, but reserved it for *Tess* (ch. xvii), where it gives Dewy (eager to avoid 'eternal welfare') and the legend itself a burlesque air more extreme than anything in the earlier novel, and quite unlike the dignity of the poem.

'In the Small Hours' (608) and 'The Country Wedding' (612), in *Late Lyrics and Earlier* (1922), unlike most of the other poems about the quire, have no connection with the Christmas season. 'In the Small Hours' has a fiddler dreaming of a long-ago wedding, where he played the tune featured at the wedding of Dick Dewy and Fancy Day. If the dreamer is Hardy himself rather than a fictional character, the music-making which he conjures up may not have belonged to the quire as such; but the feelings—love and reverence for the past people who here appear as something like fertility deities, sorrow even to tears on waking 'That Now, not Then, held reign'—are typical of poems about the quire's dead music. In 'The Country Wedding', on the other hand, these feelings are, oddly, missing. Time seems to have passed since that of the novel and most of the other poems, for William is absent. The speaker plays the treble violin, so he may be Dick Dewy. Michael, who used to play second to Reuben's tenor violin, has moved up to the tenor, Reuben plays his father's bass, and they have acquired a serpent-player, Jim, although the old quire was inclined to disapprove of serpents (I. iv). (It has been suggested that the Jim who receives punishment 'In Weatherbury Stocks' (889) may be the same man,[2] but this seems a lot to assume on the basis of two familiar local names and no mention of a serpent. It is surely more likely that Jim is Dick's younger brother, who in the novel 'made large strides like the men and did not lag behind with the other little boys': I. iv.)

The scene of 'The Country Wedding' is not Mellstock but

Weatherbury, and something seems amiss from the beginning. The weather is contradictory, the wedding party are not only most unlike the godlike one of 'In the Small Hours', but consistently at odds with the quire, though it is not entirely clear who is at fault. The bride's father addresses them apprehensively at the outset, 'Souls, for God's sake, be steady!' They quarrel with the groomsman, though with 'feelings as friends being true and hearty', and insist on walking ahead of the main group. Their cheerful tunes, kept up outside the church 'While they were swearing things none can cancel', please the bystanders but flurry the bridegroom and make the bride complain nervously, 'Too gay!' It is indeed a shock to read of a drum, so military in connotation, being beaten in the Mellstock quire. 'Your drum is a rare bowel-shaker,' said William Dewy in the novel (I. iv), who would never have permitted such goings-on. The narrator of the poem concludes by saying that the weather was, again, unusual—'foggy and fair'—when, 'in an after year', they carried the couple to church to bury them, surprisingly, both on the same day. He offers no comment, no sympathy, nor does he connect the unpropitiousness of either weather or quire with the wedding's disastrous outcome. This is a portrait of the Mellstock Quire as changed: with its gusto for life still high, but without old William, without its sense of decorum, its respect for the church, its strength of moral judgement.

Hardy took steps not to leave his readers with this memory of the quire. In *Human Shows* (1925) they are vehicles for hopefulness, either natural or religious. 'Winter Night in Woodland' (703), appearing as one of a group about snow and wintry weather, describes the pursuits of the season in 'Old Time'. In the novel the quire had the night to itself. Now the fox barking in the woods knows that the hands of all men are against it, but will never know why. Bird-baiters and poachers exercise different techniques of bagging birds 'a-perch and asleep', and smugglers pass by to hide their tubs of illicit spirits. A sound from 'dim distance' heralds the only redeeming activity in the scene: the men of the old quire, with the names of *Under the Greenwood Tree*, pass on their long rounds singing 'worn carols', the only people in the poem neither cruel, nor selfish, nor furtive, engaged on a civilized ritual for the benefit of others.

In 'The Paphian Ball' (796) the quire themselves need forgiveness for sin. The speaker is 'the tenor-viol, Michael Mail', so William is again absent. The quire carries on Christmas custom with its own sense of the past: 'We went our Christmas rounds once more, / With quire and viols as theretofore'. On this occasion, a stranger near Egdon Heath persuades them to abandon their carols to play at a mysterious party. We may remember Reuben in the novel saying 'There's always a rakish, scampish twist about a fiddle's looks that seems to say the Wicked One had a hand in making o'en' (I. iv). The quire are rescued from playing for the Devil by two miracles. Exhausted with bowing, they begin on 'While shepherds watched' by mistake. The Devil's ball room vanishes; the men find themselves on the heath. The second miracle, which has happened without their knowledge, is made clear the next morning, when they have dragged themselves to church 'shamed', only to be praised for having played, as never before, 'Rejoice, ye tenants of the earth.' This was the carol which William chose as the last of three played beneath Fancy's window in the novel. Perhaps William's faith, as well as the sound instinct which jolted them back from dance to carol, is involved in the second miracle.

Hardy had supplied the 'poetry and romance' lacking in the novel, as well as the 'deeper, more essential, more transcendant handling' which he regretted had been 'unadvisable at the date of writing . . . .'[8] The new elements he introduced into these other stories of the Mellstock musicians made poetry the only possible medium. Hardy wrote in 1915 in a letter: 'Half my time (particularly when I write verse) I believe—in the modern sense of the word—. . . in spectres, mysterious voices, intuitions, omens, dreams, haunted places, etc. etc.' (*Life*, pp. 450–51). In the poems, miraculous events cluster around those outmoded artists of simple life, who in magazine or other prose fiction could hardly sing reformingly from their graves or play at the Devil's ball. Hardy adds to the quire a spiritual dimension as well as greater understanding of purely human psychology, in the place of their narrower range of interests in the novel. In the past they represented tradition and sturdy independence, duty and joy; in the present they represent regret for the past. These were important values for Hardy, and their poetic embodiment in the quire was important and pervasive.

Despite the obstacles put in Hardy's way by publishers and

public opinion, he felt no such need to make amends to Tess in poetry as to the Mellstock Quire. He had already given her serious and respectful treatment. Yet the later novel seemed to linger in his mind and in his poems like the earlier one, to which he related it by its reference to William Dewy. The poems which relate to *Tess* do not, on the whole, narrate extra incidents as the quire poems do, but they rework novel material, singly or in groups, showing Hardy's imagination playing with the same elements to produce sometimes similar and sometimes surprisingly different effects.

Hardy began work on *Tess* in August 1889; at the end of the year he noted that 'At Middlefield Gate in February' (421) was written at 'about this time', and listed the names of the field-women of his childhood whom, at the end of the poem, he celebrates as a once blooming 'bevy now underground'. J. O. Bailey suggests that Hardy created the 'club-walking' in *Tess* partly from memories of their 'amorous play' which the poem mentions.[4] But to relate this poem too closely to chapter ii of *Tess* is a mistake. There, all the women of the village parade in white in the month of May; men join them only at a later stage of the proceedings. 'At Middlefield Gate' contrasts the wet of February with the strawy dryness of harvest; the women of the poem are those who bore the harvest labour, along with the men, 'In curtained bonnets and light array'. It is in chapter xiv, in the August after her baby's birth, that Tess goes to work binding sheaves in a company whose more interesting half is the feminine, and from whom she hides her face 'below the curtain of her bonnet'. In this chapter, as in the poem, Hardy captures the field-women's tough sensuousness, their embodiment of the fruitful season: these qualities, rising in his memory as he began work on *Tess*, may have contributed to its general plan. 'We Field Women' (866), another poem which contrasts the bleak and the joyful seasons, relates to Tess's work at Flintcomb-Ash later in the novel. In chapter xli Tess is 'compelled to don the wrapper of a field-woman', to harvest starve-acre swedes instead of corn; later she adds a 'curtained hood'. The poem's first two stanzas evoke the harsh tasks of swede hacking and reed drawing, described in greater detail in the novel; the third recounts a return to the 'laughing meads' of the dairy, which in the novel never happens. But Marian says that by talking of Talbothays and Angel Clare they could 'make it all come back a'most, in seeming' (chapter xliii). The poem's last stanza itself is like such a 'seeming', in which after rain and snow the sun shines and love is restored, in the natural rhythm of life from which Tess is tragically cut off.

These two poems on labouring women relate clearly and unambiguously to the novel. 'The Bullfinches' (86) provides a strange, indistinct parallel to scenes in which Tess tends Mrs. d'Urberville's poultry and whistles to her finches, and Alec begins to flirt with her. Mother Nature in the poem lives in a 'handsome house'; she works 'dreaming' and with 'groping' hands, as if blind. Mrs. d'Urberville, blind, called by her son a 'queer old soul', lives on a 'snug property' where everything is 'bright, thriving, and well kept' (chapter v). In both prose and verse the bullfinches are 'bulleys' or 'bullies'; in the poem they resolve to use their short time to the full in singing. One of them in the poem has been in Blackmoor Vale, from which Tess in the novel has just come, and which both poem and novel connect with fairies (chapter i). Nature never tries to protect her charges and 'unknows' or 'unheeds' how they fare, while Mrs. d'Urberville cares deeply about her pets and carefully supervises their welfare. She is, however, no protection to Tess when her evil fate is just approaching; her dying wish that her son should right the wrong he has done to Tess leads directly to his inflicting further wrongs (chapter xlvi). The poem cannot help but make her, the mother of the novel's mischief-maker, appear a distorted parody of Mother Nature, a symbolic meaning which the novel itself seems not entirely willing to bear.

Hardy wrote various poems on seduction and illegitimacy, which tend towards at least some slight connection with *Tess*. As Tess after her seduction feels herself frowned on by people and by 'some vague ethical being whom she could not class definitely as the God of her childhood', so the girl in 'After the Club-Dance' (196) ('Time's Laughingstocks III') feels herself frowned on by Blackdown Hill. The girl in the poem wonders to feel shame even before the birds who, 'too, have done the same!' In the novel Hardy has to provide an authorial voice to point out that Tess has broken 'no law known to the environment in which she fancied herself such an anomaly' (chapter xiii). The pregnant girl in 'A Sunday Morning Tragedy' (155) is unlike Tess in most ways, having a seducer she loves and an anxious loving mother—whose care, however, only procures her unnecessary death. But the girl is called by her lover 'my bird', as Tess is so often associated with birds, and is pronounced 'wronged, sinless' as Tess is 'pure'; the mother also resembles Tess in her eagerness to take all guilt on herself. Through this heart-breaking ballad runs the theme of pained amazement that 'ill-motherings'—pregnancies, whether in sheep or humans, that call for abortion—should ever be. The unmarried mother in 'The Dark-Eyed Gentleman' (201) is a resilient character who does not regret her 'slip': her child is 'My own dearest joy . . . comrade, and friend', her seducer smugly remembered as 'his daddy'. When she says of her child 'No sorrow brings he', this woman reminds us that her relationship to Tess, who names her child Sorrow, is one of contrast; but Hardy makes it clear that Tess shares her natural resilience and might, in different circumstances, have shared her happiness. 'But for the world's opinion, those experiences would have been simply a liberal education' (chapter xv). The mother in 'The Christening' (214) perhaps parallels an earlier stage in those experiences: despite her 'feverish furtive air' she has dressed her baby in the finest available and seems to accept uncomplainingly its father's choice not to marry but 'To be together / At will, just now and then.' 'Rake-hell Muses' (656) tells a similar story from the point of view of the man, who believes that the woman who has borne his child is better off without him. The lines 'I judge then, better far / She now have sorrow' recall again the name of Tess's child; this seducer feels certain that sorrow will be replaced by serenity. In 'The Dead Bastard' (857) the mother laments the loss of the child which in life was such shame and grief that she wished to be rid of it, as Tess forgets, when her baby falls ill, his 'offence against society in coming into the world . . . her soul's desire was to continue that offence by preserving the life of the child.' The field-women had not believed her when she said she wished 'the baby and her too were in the churchyard' (chapter xiv). The mother in the poem is radicalized by bereavement; of Tess Hardy says her 'passing corporeal blight had been her mental harvest' (chapter xix). Hardy could explore further in poetry what he could state in the novel ('Let the truth be told—women do as a rule live through such humiliations, and regain their spirits'), but could not develop imaginatively. Fiction demanded that the humiliations be viewed at least partly in the terms of those who inflicted them.

Poems like 'To an Unborn Pauper Child' (91) and 'The Unborn' (235), in which Hardy writes of the foetus as eager to begin life because ignorant of its wretched conditions, perhaps recall Tess's baby and also her brothers and sisters, 'six helpless creatures, who had never been asked if they wished for life on any terms, much less if they wished for it on such hard conditions as were involved in being of the shiftless house of Durbeyfield'. More generally, this theme is important in *Tess*, where the heroine has her own life gradually rendered bitter to her, and after her marriage can 'hear a penal sentence in the fiat, "You shall be born," particularly if addressed to potential issue of hers' (chapters iii, xxxvi).

The novel's idyllic chapters at Talbothays are reflected in some interesting poems. 'The Milkmaid' (126) offers a two-fold vision of a girl milking a cow. A passerby of romantic inclination might admire the scene and imagine the girl at one with Nature, that her sorrow is sorrow for the offences of Man against the countryside. In fact, her eminently natural feelings are quite different—jealous anxiety about her faithless young man and delayed new dress. The romantic passerby would be wrong in rather the same way as Angel is when, in the idyllic setting of the dairy, he says to himself, 'What a fresh and virginal daughter of Nature that milkmaid is!' (chapter xviii). 'The Head Above the Fog' (423) evokes the days when Tess and Angel rose at dawn to bring cows in from fields through 'the faint summer fogs in layers' and 'his companion's face, which was the focus of his eyes, rising above the mist stratum, seemed to have a sort of phosphorescence upon it. She looked ghostly, as if she were merely a soul at large', as well as the way that Tess before her wedding 'knew that Angel was close to her; all the rest was a luminous mist' (chapters xx, xxxii). In the poem the ghostly appearance of the warm living body is only a memory, the body too being dead and gone. Since the speaker remembers his love as 'that which once could breathe and plead!— / Skimming along with spectre-speed / To a last tryst with me', he seems to have been at fault in some breaking-off, in a manner which recalls Angel. It is as if Hardy remained dissatisfied with having given, in the novel, Angel's present feelings, and wished to express also those which he might have had in after years.

Other poems relate to the crucial days Tess spends with Angel at Wellbridge. Hardy used again the incident of the lovers' hands touching under water, again giving it very different associations from the poem 'Under the Waterfall', for Tess is anxious to please and fearful of giving offence. 'Heredity' (363) traces the inhuman immortality of 'the family face'; the poet's brooding thought is a sinister one to the novelist, who makes Angel recognize that Tess's 'fine features were unquestionably traceable in [the] exaggerated forms' of the hideously depicted d'Urberville women (chapter xxxiv). There seems also to be a connection between the portraits and 'The Caricature' (731), composed at about the same time. In this poem a young man breaks his enslavement to an older woman, Lady Lu—who has had affairs with many but who really loves him—by a cruel caricature, which, however, he never shows her. In the novel Angel has extricated himself from the clutches of an older woman before he meets Tess. After Tess's revelation, the sight of one of the portraits of the d'Urberville women, caricatures of her, prevents him from yielding to the impulse to wake her and possibly to relent (chapter xxxv); in a larger sense, the impure Tess whom Angel rejects is his ugly caricature of her. The poem reads like a testing out, in different combinations, of some of the elements in the story.

In this chapter Hardy sends his new-married, estranged pair out in the middle of the night to walk 'very slowly, without converse, one behind the other, as in a funeral procession', and invents a cottager, out late to fetch the doctor, who is impressed by their appearance and even more on his return at seeing them still 'in the same field, progressing just as slowly'. Hardy seems to have been using, for the cottager, feelings aroused in himself during his years of London residence by a 'mysterious tragic pair', silently pacing on a wet night, whom later he described in 'Beyond the Last Lamp' (257). In the poem the couple, twice seen, 'Moving slowly, moving sadly', provokes his fascinated speculation. The lane where he saw them does not exist for him without them; so long as the lane remains, they will be there 'brooding on their pain', fixed in time and space as Tess and Angel are caught in the timelessness of the novel.

Tess's pain is again vividly recalled by 'The Blinded Bird' (375). Hardy describes her patience under Angel's treatment: 'she sought not her own; was not provoked; thought no evil of his treatment of her. She might just now have been Apostolic Charity herself returned to a self-seeking modern world' (chapter xxxvi). The bird, 'Blinded ere yet a-wing' to improve its singing, provokes the questions:

> Who hath charity? This bird.
> Who suffereth long and is kind,
> Is not provoked, though blind . . .?
> Who thinketh no evil, but sings?
> Who is divine? This bird.

Tess also sings in her unhappiness, hoping that one day Angel will return and hear her (chapter xlix). The reader may feel unwilling to accept Tess's charity as a natural rather than a moral or religious quality, as it is in the poem. In this case the relation of poem with novel consists of a double parallel (Tess with Charity, the bird with Charity) whose implications are hard to fathom.

Another poem seems to retain some circumstances of an incident in the novel and to transform others. 'The Dear' (226) reminds the reader of the man who greeted Tess with 'my pretty maid' as she made her way towards Flintcomb-Ash, went on to torment her with references to her past (chapter xli), and turned out finally to be her harsh new employer. Tess, entirely unprotected, rejects and defies this persecutor. The poem's speaker meets on that same road 'A maiden one fain would guard / From every hazard and every care', who rejects the greeting 'my Dear' with its claim to protectiveness, and tells him 'with proud severity' that she is not his, but the dear of 'One far from his native land' (as Angel by this stage of the novel is in Brazil). Hardy seems to be writing in verse a meeting for Tess with a different and more sensitive admirer.

'The Lost Pyx' (140) tells a legend (which recalls the kneeling animals in 'The Oxen') associated with a stone of unknown origin on Batcombe Hill, near Dorchester. In the novel the place is sinister: Alec, who thinks the stone was once a holy cross, makes Tess swear upon it not to tempt him again; a shepherd tells her the stone is a thing of ill omen, commemorating a man who sold his soul to the devil, although others believe it merely a boundary mark. This is the day in Tess's life that starts in motion the events of the final disaster, a fatal boundary indeed for her. The poem, although its opening stanza, like the novel, puts forward contradictory possible explanations for the stone, goes on to make it commemorate a happy miracle: its triumph of both faith and nature opposes the novel's tragedy of unfulfilment.

'Tess's Lament', through its title the poem most closely connected with the novel, immediately follows 'The Lost Pyx' in *Poems of the Past and Present* (1901). It seems not to belong to any one particular moment in the narrative: Tess vividly anticipates the date of her death after that of her baby (chapter xv), and wishes for death many times (chapters xiv, xli, lii, lvi, lviii). The poem, however (which gives her none of the resilience that Hardy in the novel allowed to spring up again and again after many cruel blows), expresses a simple, pure, unmixed sorrow without any of the intricacy which in the novel characterizes motives for regret. In it, as in the letter which she writes to Angel (chapter xlviii), Tess blames herself entirely and her husband not at all. The poem distils the essential centre of her deepest emotion—yet, paradoxically, it makes her less the individual Tess and more the type of forsaken suffering womanhood.

This does not exhaust the list of poems connected with *Tess* by image or detail. 'At a Lunar Eclipse' (79) makes a comparison that Hardy uses in this novel among others, about the place of detail in the whole picture. The earth's peaks and valleys, its 'moil and misery' vanish in the serene and symmetrical shadow it casts upon the moon. The experienced stranger who met Angel in Brazil, and told him plainly that he was wrong to leave Tess, commented that 'deviations from the social norm, so immense to domesticity, were no more than are the irregularities of vale and mountain-chain to the whole terrestrial curve' (chapter xlix). 'The Wound' (397) compares the setting sun to 'that wound of mine / Of which none knew', as Tess, cruelly hurt by a tale of seduction which everyone else finds funny, feels that 'The evening sun was now ugly to her, like a great inflamed wound in the sky' (chapter xxi). The cobwebs at Flintcomb-Ash, made visible only 'by the crystallizing atmosphere' of frost, and then compared to 'white worsted' (chapter xliii), reappear with the same observation and simile in 'A Light Snow-Fall after Frost' (702). But the most striking example is 'Proud Songsters' (816: quoted in full above, p. 18). The particle from which this singing arose is clearly a sentence in *Tess*:

> Another year's instalment of flowers, leaves, nightingales, thrushes, finches, and such ephemeral creatures, took up their positions where only a year ago others had stood in their place when these were nothing more than germs and inorganic particles.
> (chapter xx)

The sentence is whimsical and pleasing, a contribution to the novel's preoccupation with themes of fertility and of change; but beside the poem it appears to lack individual life, it is inorganic. The comparison might cause a reader hastily to conclude that the Muse of Song is superior to that of Story. But Hardy's own view is wiser. To re-read *Under the Greenwood Tree* or *Tess* after reading the poems connected with them is to be impressed anew by the energy of the novels' more diffused life, as well as to realise that the poems have, almost imperceptibly, made significant alterations in the way in which the novels are read.

NOTES

1. Preface to *Under the Greenwood Tree* (1912, Wessex Edition), p. x.
2. J. O. Bailey, *The Poetry of Thomas Hardy, A Handbook and Commentary* (Chapel Hill, North Carolina, 1970), p. 611.
3. Preface to *Under the Greenwood Tree*, p. x.
4. Bailey, p. 381.

5

Thoughts from Sophocles: Hardy in the '90s

by JEREMY V. STEELE

The 1890s saw Hardy at last achieving a public transition from
prose to poetry. But it was not achieved comfortably: there are
strong indications that during the decade he came to feel increasingly isolated, doubtful and depressed. His unhappiness and the
crisis in his writing career mirror each other, and it is, I believe,
illuminating to consider them in the light of his response to the
two plays of Sophocles based on the Oedipus legend. For, so far
as one can tell from the surviving evidence, he was more deeply
affected by the Oedipus plays during the 1890s than at any other
period of his life, and he seems to have found within them images
of his own distress.

A note from 1889, just at the edge of the decade, which reflects
his perusal of a library copy of Jebb's edition of *Oedipus
Tyrannus*, is comparatively well-known.

> *July* 24. B. Museum:
> Εἰ δέ τι πρεσβύτερον, etc. Soph. *Oed. Tyr.* 1365 ('and if there
> be a woe surpassing woes, it hath become the portion of Oedi-
> pus'—Jebb. Cf. Tennyson: 'a deeper deep').[1]

It is, however, rather less well-known that a few years later he
acquired his own copy of Jebb's *Oedipus Tyrannus* (the third
edition of 1893), perhaps encouraged to do so by an enthusiastic
review article which his friend, S. H. Butcher, had included in
Some Aspects of the Greek Genius (1891).[2] Jebb edited all the
plays of Sophocles in similar style, with a translation facing the
text and an extensive commentary below, but *Oedipus Tyrannus*
is the only one of the series Hardy is known to have possessed.
Indeed it is the only full-dress scholarly edition of a single Greek
play in a separate volume recorded from his library, and the

acquisition in itself suggests unusual interest. Doubtless he was already familiar with the play—he may even have started on it in the Greek as early as 1860-61[3]—but one would not guess from the scattered markings in his Bohn translation (which include an unusual proportion of added stage-directions) that it held any particular significance for him.[4]

The markings in his copy of Jebb are probably later than those on the Bohn version and are certainly more frequent: they cover some twenty-five passages in the Greek, and often the corresponding English too. Altogether they suggest a more acute response to the play, and a fresh kindling of his interest in Oedipus is apparent in an important change to the text of *The Return of the Native* which he made in 1895. For seventeen years Clym Yeobright's expression on emerging from his inquisition of Johnny Nunsuch had been described thus:

> The pupils of his eyes, fixed steadfastly on blankness, were vaguely lit with an icy shine; his mouth had passed into the phase more or less imaginatively rendered in studies of Laocoon.
>
> (V.2 ad fin.)

In revising the text for the first collected edition of his novels Hardy substituted Oedipus for Laocoon, but left the rest of the sentence unaltered, so transforming a firmly placed visual image into one with portentous literary associations which Clym cannot sustain. It is not as though the rendering of Laocoon's face in the famous Vatican sculpture had lost its suggestiveness, for he had just revived the image within a page or two of the end of Part Second in *Jude the Obscure*, but Oedipus had apparently penetrated his imagination far enough to compel a change that does not sit easily either in its immediate context or in the wider spans of the book.

Hardy's study of his Jebb in the '90s is confirmed by the dating of a marked line (121), where Oedipus, suddenly faced with the formidable task of discovering who killed Laius years beforehand, presses Creon for a scrap of information: 'One thing might show the clue to many, could we get but a small beginning for hope.' Underlining the second clause only in the Greek and the English, Hardy added 'August, 1897' in the margin. Such dates usually register some personal significance, and there is little doubt that here he detached the line from its place in the drama and applied it to the particularly deep and persistent depression which found voice in his three 'In Tenebris' poems. The second he dated 1895–96, and the third 1896; the first is undated but clearly belonged with the others in his mind. Its final stanza suggests why he isolated 'could we get but a small beginning for hope'.

> Black is night's cope;
> But death will not appal
> One who, past doubtings all,
>   Waits in unhope.   (136)

His depression in the '90s cannot be set down to any single cause and a full understanding of it will, I suspect, always prove elusive. But it is clear from the printed text of the *Life*, and still more from deleted passages preserved in the TSS, that he was deeply hurt by the reception of his last three novels, especially *Jude the Obscure*. After reading one review of *Tess of the d'Urbervilles* he eased his feelings in a note which ends: ' ". . . Well, if this sort of thing continues no more novel-writing for me. A man must be a fool to deliberately stand up to be shot at." '[5] None the less in *Jude* and *The Well-Beloved* he went on to expose more of himself and his intimate concerns than ever before, to find the revelations greeted by some as obscene. The hostility he aroused shocked him and, always over-sensitive to criticism, he began to suspect persecution. It seemed now that poetry could give him more shelter and more freedom to write what he wanted; and even at the beginning of the decade, before he had experienced the most virulent attacks upon him, he had anticipated the release it might bring.

> *Christmas Day* [1890]. While thinking of resuming 'the viewless wings of poesy' before dawn this morning, new horizons seemed to open, and worrying pettinesses to disappear. . . .
>
> (*Life*, p. 230)

A year later he was planning a volume to be called 'Songs of Five-and-Twenty Years'. But he was well aware of the difficulties he faced in breaking through the reputation he had as a novelist exclusively, and his resentment of the barrier continued to show long afterwards. He was also uncertain of his poetic gifts and 'at first with some consternation he had found an awkwardness in getting back to an easy expression in numbers after abandoning it for so many years' (*Life*, p. 292). It was thus a critical and painful time for him as a writer: even though the commercial success of *Tess* and *Jude* and the publication of the first collected edition of the novels must have given him some financial security, he was unsettled in his future direction. His recent achievements were tainted by their reception, he felt a need to win fresh ground, and *The Dynasts* revolved in his mind vast and unattempted. 'How to speak, I know not; I am fluttered with forebodings; neither in the present have I clear vision, nor of the future.' These lines from *Oedipus Tyrannus* (485–86) show the Chorus frightened and bewildered by what they have heard Teiresias tell Oedipus, but when Hardy marked them in the Greek and (with more emphasis) in the English, he may have seen in them a reflection of his own disquiet.

Besides such springs of worry and depression in his professional life, inseparable from his estimate of himself and the urge to express faithfully his personal experience and vision, he was confronted by a growing estrangement from his wife (whose distaste for *Jude* has not always been given the understanding it deserves). At the same time he had to weather hopeless attractions towards other women like Florence Henniker and Agnes Grove, and he must have asked himself what the future could bring to one held in a souring and apparently indissoluble union. In September 1896 the couple revisited Flanders for the first time since the second year of their marriage, and at the end of a letter to Florence Henniker he obliquely measured the experience. 'It is 20 years since I was last in this part of Europe, and the reflection is rather saddening. I ask myself, why am I here again, and not underground.'[6] The belief that his proper place was underground was shaped into a poem, 'The Dead Man Walking' (166), that same year. It traces some of the stages in his gradual, scarcely perceived progress into the shadow of death, where he pictures himself merely sustaining a charade.

> Yet is it that, though whiling
>   The time somehow
> In walking, talking, smiling,
>   I live not now.

One may wonder whether his marking of the end of Oedipus'

prayer in the Bohn version of *Oedipus Coloneus* (p. 58) dates from this time: 'compassionate this woe-begone phantom of a man in Oedipus; for indeed this is not my original frame.'

The sense of having died to life also underlies the numb despair of 'In Tenebris I', but in the second poem of the group it gives place to his sense of being a pariah, with no place among the assertive throngs of optimists who breezily assume, 'All's well with us: ruers have nought to rue!' (137). Oppressed, he momentarily questions how far the truth is with them, but the final stanza asserts his much bleaker, sterner vision without apology. The conviction of utter isolation from his fellows reappears in 'Wessex Heights' (261), dated 1896, but there it extends to infect his past as well. Below the hill-crests to which he escapes he is dogged by the phantoms of people whom he knew in earlier times:

> They hang about at places, and they say harsh heavy things—
> Men with a wintry sneer, and women with tart disparagings.

Even his former self, 'my simple self that was', haunts him with accusations of betrayal. The profound alienation that scars these poems seems to have found some pattern in the fallen Oedipus. The final lines of *Oedipus Tyrannus*, given to the Chorus, point to the superbly sharp and dramatic example of peripeteia that Oedipus represents and to the fragility of human happiness—a theme Hardy had noticed earlier (1186–96). They begin thus:

> Dwellers in our native Thebes, behold, this is Oedipus, who knew the famed riddle, and was a man most mighty; on whose fortunes what citizen did not gaze with envy?

Hardy double-lined the Greek in the margin of his Jebb and added a cross-reference to Isaiah 14.16, which reads:

> They that see thee shall narrowly look upon thee, and consider thee, saying, Is this the man that made the earth to tremble, that did shake kingdoms . . .?

Obviously he did not see himself as a fallen king, either of Thebes or Babylon: in 'Wessex Heights' he finds his liberty in ascent (and perhaps the poem glances at the heights of Parnassus as well). But he had no doubt that he was narrowly looked upon: 'Down there they are dubious and askance; there nobody thinks as I'. His vulnerable awareness of having become notorious, a figure to be pointed at and shunned, can be felt behind the additional underlining in both Greek and English of 'behold, this is Oedipus', and 'Nay, to the gods I have become most hateful' (Oedipus' claim five lines above). It would, however, be as absurd to suppose he endorsed this literally as to look for detailed Oedipal parallels in his life: the parallels are rather to be seen in his having reached a vision of self and the human condition almost overwhelmingly different from that commonly prevailing, in feeling the thrust of that difference from the community about him, and in simultaneously fearing and seeking the rejection of himself as an alien.

> Let him in whose ears the low-voiced Best is killed by the clash
>   of the First . . .
> Get him up and be gone as one shaped awry; he disturbs the
>   order here.
>
> ('In Tenebris II')

His wish that he had died while still a child, 'artless, unrueing', which forms the substance of 'In Tenebris III' (138), also has a parallel in the complaints of Oedipus against his rescue from the fatal exposure to which his parents had condemned him as an infant (1349–55, 1391–93). But Hardy did not mark either passage, and his regret that he was spared for his adult experience is marked by a more measured sadness than comes from the anguish of Oedipus. Another poem probably begun in this period was, however, very firmly based in a closely related passage from *Oedipus Coloneus*, where the Chorus of old men, who have witnessed the traumatic shocks that still assail the aged and outcast Oedipus, reflect upon the pain of prolonged life. Hardy tried his hand at condensing it to sonnet-form, apparently in 1895 when his depression was already established. But he seems never to have taken it beyond draft stage and 'Thoughts from Sophocles' (924) remained unpublished until 1956.

> Who would here sojourn for an outstretched spell
> Has senseless promptings, to the thinking gaze,
> Since pain comes nigh and nigher with lengthening days,
> And nothing shows that joy will ever upwell.

Death is the remedy that cures at call
The doubtful jousts of black and white assays.
What are song, laughter, what the footed maze,
Beside the good of knowing no birth at all?

Gaunt age is as some blank upstanding beak
Chafed by the billows of a northern shore
And facing friendless cold calamity
That strikes upon its features worn and weak
Where sunshine bird and bloom frequent no more,
And cowls of cloud wrap the stars' radiancy.[7]

Some verbal echoes suggest that Hardy worked from the English version in his Bohn Sophocles, and his rather vague source-reference, 'Oed. Col. 1200–1250', may have been guessed from the running heads there, but it is the star image in the final line which confirms it as his source. As Evelyn Hardy observed, 'Neither in the original, nor in the renderings of Jebb, Housman, and other translators, is there any mention of the stars.' However, the image is not, as she claimed, 'a personal transmutation, a softening of Sophoclean gloom', for Hardy took it from the Bohn version, where T. A. Buckley explained in a footnote that the Greek suggested to him 'the weak, uncertain light of the stars struggling through the clouds on a dark night.' And since Hardy evidently worked from this version rather than the Greek, it seems worth giving here to see more clearly what he did with it.

CHORUS. Whoever seeks to live for a lengthened term, neglecting the mean, will be proved in my mind to cherish folly; since oft has length of days brought us nearer to pain, and you can no where see aught of joy when any one may meet with more than his wishes require; but death is the aid (of our troubles) that ends with the grave, when that fate hath appeared without nuptial hymn, without lyre, or dance, and death to close the scene. Not to have been born at all is superior to every view of the question; and this when one may have seen the light, to return thence whence he came as quickly as possible, is far the next best. For when youth comes bringing light follies, who wanders without the pale of many sorrows?—what suffering is not there?—murders, factions, strife, battle, and envy: and loathsome old age hath gained the last scene,—impotent, unsociable, friendless old age, where all ills, worst of ills, dwell together. In which state this wretched man, not I alone, as some promontory exposed to the north, is beaten on all sides by the dashings of the billows in the winter storm;—thus also dreadful calamities, bursting like waves over his head, ever present beat on him,—some indeed from the setting of the sun, and some from his rise, and some from his mid-day beam, and some from the cloud-dimmed stars of night.[8]

Hardy's first stanza follows his model quite closely; indeed the paraphrase is close enough to bring to mind the interlinear technique he used in versifying some of his prose sources for *The Dynasts*.[9] In the second stanza, however, he compressed and varied freely, even wildly, which is partly to be attributed to the way that the translation darkens the obscurities of a corrupt text. Faced with a confused progression in the argument he resolved his own, reserving for its climax the clearest point, that not to be born is best. But the idea of suicide, introduced as an ever-present option with 'cures at call', is foreign to the Chorus' meditation on endurance, as he recognized in the uncancelled variant 'winds up well'. 'The doubtful jousts of black and white assays' seems to call rather desperately on the chess-board to cover the Sophoclean catalogue of life's ills, while its pleasures, 'song, laughter [and] the footed maze', apparently derive from the inversion of death's appearance 'without nuptial hymn, without lyre, or dance'.

In the sestet Hardy moved closer to his model again but still varied and ornamented it freely, gathering in some material (e.g. 'impotent, unsociable, friendless old age') from outside the simile proper. Understandably he suppressed references to Oedipus and the old men of the Chorus to make the image absolute and universal. The variant 'gray' pencilled above 'blank' in the opening line shows him uncertain whether to emphasize the human or the inanimate elements in the fusion, and a similar uncertainty underlies interpretation of the last four lines of the Greek: do the positions of the sun denote points of the compass (which slants the image to the cliff) or do they measure a man's growth and decline? Following Buckley's preference for the second alternative, Hardy narrowed it to an equation of old age with starless night. However, particularly in the penultimate line, which has scarcely any foundation in the original, he may also have had in mind Shakespeare's 73rd sonnet, 'That time of year thou mayst in me behold'. With similar intent it offers images of early winter: leafless boughs 'which shake against the cold, / Bare ruin'd choirs where late the sweet birds sang'; twilight fading into night, 'Death's second self that seals up all in rest'—which is of course close to Hardy's 'Death is the remedy that winds up well'.

Although the sestet—too heavily alliterated, yet merging the features of the old man and the sea-cliff in subtle re-creation—is the only part of the sonnet which reaches for distinction, it remains surprising that Hardy never published the whole: for instance in the short section of 'Imitations, etc.' in *Poems of the Past and the Present*, since it is not inferior to the version of Catullus XXXI which he did include there. But perhaps he put it aside for further work and polishing and then overlooked it; perhaps he was always dissatisfied with the compression in the second stanza—a problem endemic in the form he had chosen. He seems not to have made a similar attempt elsewhere in Greek drama, though on 1 March 1897, not so long after the probable date of the draft, he noted an intention to make a lyric of another passage from Sophocles—the closing lines of the *Trachiniae*, which for him were a *locus classicus* of protest against the ordering of the world (*Life*, pp. 285, 383). However, by his own reckoning he never carried it out, and he was possibly satisfied by working the core of the protest into *The Dynasts*, which he did comparatively soon in the complaint of the Pities after the death of Nelson (I.v.4 ad fin.).

It is significant that both the passages he chose to work on run directly counter to the received opinions he reproduced in 'In Tenebris II'.

> Our times are blessed times, they cry: Life shapes it as is most
>   meet,
> And nothing is much the matter; there are many smiles to a
>   tear;
> Then what is the matter is I, I say. Why should such an one
>   be here? . . .

Yet the doubting of his place in the world, the instinct for absolute retreat which governs this group of poems, was balanced and ultimately overweighed by an urge to declare his dissenting vision of Life, which at times verged on a sense of prophetic mission. It had surfaced irregularly through his career as a novelist, from its beginnings in the tart radicalism of *The Poor Man and the Lady* until its virtual end in *Jude*. His note of 28 April 1888, which he thought preserved the germ of *Jude*, also states this missionary sense with unusual clarity: ' "... There is something [in this] the world ought to be shown, and I am the one to show it to them ..." ' (*Life*, p. 208; Hardy's square brackets). But, as we have noticed, he was not prepared for the violence of some reactions to what he had to show there, and the problem of what to say and how to say it became. acute.

The Sophoclean pattern of his dilemma is to be traced not so much in Oedipus himself as in the blind seer, Teiresias. Admittedly Oedipus, set apart by the terrible things he has done, also becomes in the later play an awesome figure, of mysterious destiny and power, but in *Oedipus Tyrannus* he is the victim, not the vessel of knowledge. That part is reserved to Teiresias, who suddenly finds himself in the position of knowing all that Oedipus wants to know and knowing equally that it is too awful to tell. The realisation is enshrined in his opening words: 'Alas, how dreadful to have wisdom where it profits not the wise!' (316-17) Here in Jebb Hardy marked the Greek and the English, adding a cross-reference to Gray; he was recalling the end of 'Ode on a Distant Prospect of Eton College'.

> No more; where ignorance is bliss,
> 'Tis folly to be wise.[10]

Clearly Teiresias' exclamation echoed his own conviction, frequently expressed (in 'Before Life and After', for example), that human self-consciousness has evolved in severe disproportion to human suffering. But the likelihood that it also held a more specific meaning for him as a writer with unpalatable truths to tell is strongly suggested by his attention to a similar scene in the *Phoenissae* of Euripides, where Teiresias tells Creon that one of his sons must be sacrificed to preserve the city of Thebes. It is characteristic of the different quality of the two plays that this scene is much less tautly written than Sophocles' explosive encounter; none the less Hardy fastened upon Teiresias' rejoinder to Creon's hectic dismissal of him and his prophecies: 'Has truth perished, because thou art unfortunate?' The unusually heavy marking of this acid question is picked up by a lighter one against the prophet's departing sentence on his art: whoever practises it is a fool, for if he has disagreeable things to tell he must either make himself hated or, out of pity for those affected, be false to his divine inspiration.[11] Hardy's loyalty was to the truths perceived within himself, not to any supernaturally revealed, but he was equally perturbed by pressure to compromise their utterance. In 'Lausanne: In Gibbon's Old Garden: 11-12 p.m.' (72), a poem prompted by a visit there in June 1897, he used the ghost of Gibbon to deplore the crab-wise advance of truth, and the obliqueness of the device seconds his complaint.

> . . . May one not speed her but in phrase askance?
> Do scribes aver the Comic to be Reverend still? . . .

(The suppression of Gibbon's 'ironically civil' undermining of the Church in William Smith's abridgement of the *Decline and Fall* was a doubled irony that would not have been lost on him.)[12] The conclusion of the poem draws together a little community of truth-tellers across two and a half centuries, with Gibbon quoting Milton versified by Hardy:

> Still rule those minds on earth
> At whom sage Milton's wormwood words were hurled:
> *'Truth like a bastard comes into the world*
> *Never without ill-fame to him who gives her birth'*?[13]

Hardy's sense of identity with Teiresias under the burden of knowledge, or truth, was perhaps reinforced by seeing an analogue of the attacks upon himself in the blind anger of Oedipus, who, to fend off the truths he fears, hits back at Teiresias with absurd accusations of conspiracy. Certainly it was the menace of his assailants which shaped a note he made on 17 October 1896, soon after returning from Flanders.

> Poetry. Perhaps I can express more fully in verse ideas
> and emotions which run counter to the inert crystallized
> opinion—hard as a rock—which the vast body of men have
> vested interests in supporting. . . . (*Life*, p. 284)

The continuation, which anticipates almost with relish the vituperative reaction that a prose argument of his views would arouse, concentrates on the expression of heterodox *ideas* in verse. For some years to come he was much occupied with such endeavours, and not only in *The Dynasts*, though that stands as the largest monument to his life-long effort to understand the system of which he found himself a tiny and transient part. In 1920 he closed a contentious correspondence with Alfred Noyes thus: ' "... The Scheme of Things is, indeed, incomprehensible; and there I suppose we must leave it—perhaps for the best. Knowledge might be terrible." ' (*Life*, p. 410) The final thrust was not merely rhetorical; his vision hesitated at the brink of the terrible but could not turn away from it, and in the poem he chose to end his last volume, *Winter Words*, he took the stance of a Teiresian seer who will no longer speak the dreadful things he knows.[14]

However, as he rightly judged, his ideas were rooted in his emotions, and he needed poetry not simply for its promise of greater intellectual freedom but to express the whole compass of his feeling with a pungency and directness not easily reconciled with the larger impersonative forms of the novel. Once he put away the mask of the novelist he was paradoxically more free to write of his intimate experience, for, as Robert Gittings has well observed, 'Poems could reveal more of the emotion, but less of the biographical circumstances.'[15] And as he passed into old age, and saw death nearing himself and overtaking many of the people who had mattered to him, he seems to have felt a still stronger desire to digest his experience in the making of poems. Working on compact, separate entities allowed him to set aside consistency and record freely the diversity of his moods and memories, without the constraints imposed by a larger structure.

Oedipus Tyrannus, like much of Greek tragedy, is concerned with the impact of the past upon the present; it is also concerned to an unusual degree with the problems of knowledge (though it denies any broad solutions), and it is the coming to full knowledge of his past which destroys Oedipus in the present. In 1900 Hardy picked out a passing mention of this most disturbing aspect of the play from an article on psychical research and noted it down: ' "*The terrific oracle of Oedipus*: 'Mayst thou ne'er know the truth of what thou art.' " '[16] The words are, however, almost the last ones Jocasta speaks to Oedipus, just after she has realised that he is her son—not strictly an oracle. There is no ground for presuming that Hardy was ever overturned by so sudden and terrible a revelation, even though the image of himself as utterly isolated and alienated seems to have taken on almost Oedipal dimensions in the 1890s. The greatest shock registered in his poetry is the death of his first wife in 1912, after which the knowledge that she was entirely beyond his reach, and the discovery of her early recollections and her hostile diary of their latter years, forced him very painfully back into their past. But the sequence of poems about her which so remarkably reawakens and revalues that past would not have been possible without his capacity for retaining emotional experience, which was developed to a degree that suggests his deepest reactions belonged to retrospect—or anticipation—and that he was disinclined to engage fully with anything whilst it was happening. The cliché 'living in the past' assumes fresh meaning when applied to him, and poetry proved to be the ideal medium through which to explore his memory and his mind. The act of giving an experience or an idea external existence in a poem was a means of working out and coming to terms with the feeling inseparable from it, and it is likely that his serious and immensely productive application to poetry was more important than anything else in his gradual resolution of the crisis of the '90s.

NOTES

1. *Life*, p. 220 Hardy himself was of course very largely responsible for its compilation. Tennyson's phrase was recalled from *In Memoriam* LXIII. A disclaimer of 'any possible personal reason for his quoting this at this moment' has been deleted on f.300v. of the TS (Dorset County Museum; hereafter DCM).

2. Hardy's copies of both volumes are now in the possession of Professor R. L. Purdy, and I am very grateful for his permission to refer to them here. There is a somewhat misleading description of the Jebb in W. R. Rutland, *Thomas Hardy: A Study of his Writings and their Background* (Oxford, 1938), p. 35.

3. See *Life*, p. 33; however, the TS (ff.42v.-43) shows that Hardy's memory of the details of his reading was vague, and the record of his library suggests a start on Aeschylus rather than Sophocles.

4. The Bohn Sophocles was a revision of the 'Oxford' translation by T. A. Buckley. Hardy's copy (n.d.) is now in the possession of F. B. Adams, Jr., who very kindly allows me to refer to it here. The reasons for believing that Hardy did not acquire it until the mid-'70s must be argued elsewhere.

5. *Life*, p. 246; seven sentences deleted from TS ff.339-40 in a typical toning-down of Hardy's reactions may be found in *The Personal Notebooks of Thomas Hardy*, ed. Richard H. Taylor (1978), p. 236.

6. *One Rare Fair Woman: Thomas Hardy's Letters to Florence Henniker 1893-1922*, ed. Evelyn Hardy and F. B. Pinion, (1972), p. 54.

7. In *Complete Poems* this text is supplemented by a note of uncancelled MS variants on p. 969. Evelyn Hardy printed a slightly different text in 'Some Unpublished Poems by Thomas Hardy', *The London Magazine*, 3, no. 1 (Jan. 1956), 28–39, which also includes a facsimile of the MS. Her suggestion that the '[95]' pencilled beside the title might be a page-reference to Jebb's edition of the play rather than a date has no foundation, though Hardy could have added it, with the few pencilled variants, some time later.

8. In his own copy (pp. 93–4) Hardy marginally lined the first two sentences and, more heavily, the beginning of the simile (to 'winter storm'). He additionally underlined 'Not to have been born . , . question'—a belief reportedly endorsed in an interview he gave in 1901. 'For instance, people call me a pessimist; and if it is pessimism to think, with Sophocles, that "not to have been born is best", then I do not reject the designation.' (William Archer, *Real Conversations*, 1904, p. 46) The succeeding idea of returning whence one came is echoed in the fourth line of 'Wessex Heights': 'I seem where I was before my birth, and after death may be.'

9. See, for example, plate [2] in Walter F. Wright, *The Shaping of The Dynasts* (Lincoln, Nebraska, 1967).

10. Hardy at some time entered the corresponding cross-reference against Gray's lines in the copy of Palgrave's *Golden Treasury* given to him by Horace Moule in 1862 (DCM). He also marked his Bohn translation at the same point.

11. Hardy's markings are found on pp. 112–13 of his copy of the first volume of the Bohn translation of Euripides (1850), which he acquired second-hand. It is now in the possession of F. B. Adams, Jr., who again kindly allows me to refer to it here.

12. See *Jude the Obscure*, II.1. A copy of the abridgement from the Max Gate library, *The Student's Gibbon* (1868), was listed by the First Edition Bookshop as item 117 in their catalogue 33 (November 1938).

13. *Life*, p. 294, gives Milton's original words in a footnote. They are heavily marked in Hardy's copy of vol. 3 of the Bohn *Prose Works of John Milton* (Colby College), and he entered them in his commonplace book, *Literary Notes* II (DCM), about 1894 when he was working on *Jude*—where another passage from *The Doctrine and Discipline of Divorce* forms a challenging epigraph to Part Fourth.

14. His underlining in Jebb of Teiresias' warning to Oedipus, 'thou has sight, yet seest not in what misery thou art' (413), seems to look forward to 'The blinkered sight of souls in bond', set against his own penetrating vision of the truth in this final poem, 'He Resolves to Say No More'.

15. *The Older Hardy* (1978), p. 85.

16. Entered in *Literary Notes* II from *Harper's New Monthly Magazine*, 100 (Apr. 1900), 786. Hardy also looked up Jebb's version of the line and appended it as more literal.

6

Thomas Hardy and George Meredith

by CORNELIA COOK

George Meredith met Thomas Hardy when, as Chapman and Hall's reader, he returned the manuscript of Hardy's first novel. His criticism buried *The Poor Man and the Lady*, and a further loss to Hardy was his failure to recognize in this reader the author of *Modern Love*. This long delayed Hardy's acquaintance with the man of the 'luminous countenance' whose picture was to hang in his study when both writers had traced curiously congruous paths from obscure origins to literary eminence.

Hardy's aims for a realist fiction placed him with Meredith in the ranks of embattled innovators. By the time Hardy turned his back on critical misprision and downed his fictional tools in 1897 to embrace his first love, verse, Meredith, never having escaped the stigma of obscurity in prose despite popular success, had also ended his career as a novelist. Convinced that 'it's my nature to sing'[1], he, too, published poetry until his death in 1909. Hardy's 'memorial lines' (*Life*, p. 345) caught the Meredithian note in simile and concise declaration:

> He spoke as one afoot will wind
> A morning horn ere men awake;
> His note was trenchant, turning kind.

He praised Meredith's critical insight,

> He was of those whose wit can shake
> And riddle to the very core
> The counterfeits that Time will break . . . .
>
> 'George Meredith' (243)

And significantly, he hints an immortality for Meredith, envisaging Meredith's continuing presence within the natural setting

of 'his green hill'. The presence depends on Hardy's memory of
the scene, but implies that Meredith is part of the hill, much as
Hardy saw Meredith's friend Leslie Stephen becoming part of
his hill, the Schreckhorn, when he asked,

> At his last change, when Life's dull coils unwind,
> Will he, in old love, hitherward escape,
> And the eternal essence of his mind
> Enter this silent adamantine shape . . . .

'The Schreckhorn' (264)

If Hardy is making such a suggestion about Meredith he is
nodding towards that idea of an immortality in nature which he
entertained so fitfully and Meredith so faithfully. But he sub-
sumes the vexed question of the personal in an idea of artistic
immortality, 'His words wing on—as live words will'. Perhaps
a slightly tentative note colours the formal tribute's conclusion;
Hardy did not find all of. Meredith's words 'live'. He is well
known to have commented, 'Meredith has some poetry, and yet
I can read James when I cannot look at Meredith' (*Life*, p. 370).
This 'poetry' is that in Meredith's prose. Apart from references
to the unmerited 'bludgeonings' incurred by *Modern Love* from
'reviewers who were out to suppress anything like originality',[2]
Hardy's familiarity with Meredith's poetry is undocumented.

By 1928 Hardy expected not so much that Meredith's words
would rise lark-like, as that his ideas would cleave through a
foam of verbiage. He wrote,

> The likelihood is that, after some years have passed, what was
> best in his achievement—at present partly submerged by its other
> characteristics—will rise still more distinctly to the surface than
> it has done already. Then he will not only be regarded as a writer
> who said finest and profoundest things often in a tantalising way,
> but as one whose work remains an essential portion of the vast
> universal volume which enshrines as contributors all those that
> have adequately recorded their reading of life. (*PW*, 154)

What Hardy thought finest in Meredith's achievement seems to
have been not the 'brilliancy' of style (which covered the underlying tragedy of life in a 'veil' of comic criticism, *Life*, p. 439),
but the substance—the elder man's engagement with 'profound-
est' questions. The 'words' which Hardy found most 'live' were
probably those of Meredith's conversation, in which enthusiasm

banished artificiality and Hardy discovered that Meredith 'did not forget . . . that . . . "Comedy is Tragedy if you only look deep enough" ' (*PW*, 154).

Hardy's tributes, for all their conventionality, express a deep, if complex, respect for Meredith. Dating from that first rejection, it persists in repeated allusions in the *Life* which measure Hardy's work against Meredith's 'advice'. Hardy thought he had taken this 'too literally' (p. 63); then he wished he had sought it in writing his second book ('Meredith would have . . . offered some suggestions on how to make a better use of the good material', p. 76); then he reproached (and exonerated) himself for 'too crude an interpretation of George Meredith's advice', and wondered 'What Meredith would have thought of the result of his teaching' (p. 85); later he sought Meredith's encouragement to persevere with *The Dynasts*.[3] The extraordinary nightmare of 1923 in which Hardy dreamt of himself on a ladder struggling to lift 'an infant in blue and white, bound up in a bundle' to the safety of a loft on which 'sat George Meredith in his shirt sleeves, smoking', indifferent to the fate of the child which 'was his',[4] suggests the strength and ambivalence of this respect. Its more comfortable issue was the 'calling' habit which, between 1899 and 1906, frequently drew Hardy to Meredith's cottage.

Whether Hardy actually regarded Meredith as a presider over his literary efforts we cannot know. Both men were adept at covering their autobiographical tracks, while at the same time exploiting their most intimate experiences in fiction and in poetry. But we can look for a literary relationship such as Lawrence saw when he remarked that 'Thomas Hardy and George Meredith have, to some extent, answered' Synge's call for 'the brutalising of English poetry'.[5] It is unnecessary to exaggerate 'influence', or to construct a conscious dialogue in verse between optimist and pessimist, to find the two associating themselves with similarly 'modern' subjects or ways of seeing.

As thoroughgoing naturalists both poets view a world moved only by an intrinsic impulse—Hardy's Immanent Will; Meredith's Earth—as yet remote from evolved consciousness. While both exhort 'More brain, O Lord, more brain!' (*Modern Love*, XLVIII), both respect the beast in man.[6] For the beast, often an obstacle to the perfection of consciousness, alone harbours the capacity for sensation necessary for growth towards perfection.

Lawrence recognized a truthful brutality in the way both poets dealt fearlessly and even wryly with sex and its role in shaping destinies, universal (through evolution) and personal. Both deplore the cultivated distance between sensation and intellection which induces men to thwart or stifle their most natural instincts in a materialist society. Hardy tirelessly explores the mismatchings of passion and perception accounting for a multitude of life's comic and tragic ironies—and boldly offers his public a diet of grotesques in the areas of love and death—in his bid for realism and unclouded consciousness.

Meredith recognizes sensual appetite as both the motive force of nature's continuity and the destructive ally of mortality. Urging the evolutionary need for sense to wed intellect, both writers nevertheless see potential in this union the most powerful human tragedy—the discovery that the real and the ideal are incommensurate. Reason and imagination enable men to form ideals: 'Mistress, friend, place, aims to be bettered straightway'; the senses enable their pursuit. The ideal, however, can kill the real, leaving a spoilt Amabel, a wasted shadow of the Well-Beloved, 'a phantom-woman in the Past' (*Modern Love*). Alternatively, the real—the cruelties of possession, proximity, time and mortality—can kill what was ideal of form or sentiment in itself, leaving a host of withered, embittered wrecks.

The tension between the ideal and the real—in aspiration and inadequacy—brutalizes the texture itself of these writers' poetry. Regularity coexists with irregularity; precision with innuendo or abstraction; profundity or magnitude with flippancy and triviality in a Gothic savageness. Hardy and Meredith are perhaps the latest children of the Gothic Revival which re-discovered the virtues of an architecture, and thence an art, aspiring to the supernatural by way of the copied forms of the natural, which raised 'out of fragments full of imperfection, and betraying that imperfection in every touch'[7] edifices of beauty and integrity. The style to which Ruskin assigned the requisites of Savageness, Changefulness, Naturalism, Grotesqueness, Rigidity and Redundance appealed to poetic naturalists and evolutionists who recognized imperfection as indigenous to nature, and change as nature's life-force.

Gothic churches were Hardy's study and work as architect and restorer. In his fantasy on the invention of the 'Perpendicular'

Style ('The Abbey Mason') Hardy ascribes the inspiration of the style to nature, its inception to a need for progress in the art, and he sees the art realize an ideal beyond imagination ('achievement distancing desire'). Such a need for 'new forms' was one of Hardy's own motives for imitating the eclectic and ornamental style of Gothic architecture in *The Dynasts* in his attempt to represent nature in its real aspects, 'men's lives and actions', and to pursue the ideal, 'things behind'.

Meredith encountered the Gothic when he became a schoolboy in the Rhineland in the year that German nationalism declared its own rebirth symbolized in the restoration of Cologne cathedral. Meredith continued unhistorically to associate Gothicism with Teutonism; he loved the 'wild weird [German] humour . . . that yet . . . excites laughter even while the hair is on end', and his own woodland poems are in spirit offshoots of the wonderful *Märchen* informed by 'implicit faith in those ancient forests of Rhineland and Westphalia'.[8]

One finds those principles of Gothic architecture which Hardy sought to translate into the poetic medium—'cunning irregularity . . . the principle of spontaneity . . . resulting in the "unforeseen" . . . character of his metres and stanzas, . . . poetic texture rather than poetic veneer' (*Life*, p. 301)—realized in a number of practices which he shares with Meredith. Although both are precise in rendering classical syllabic metres into English equivalents, it is ultimately through pronounced rhythms that both achieve the changeful monotony which Ruskin associated with nature's sublime manifestations in land and sea-scape. Hardy's rhythms can be significantly awkward. The 'sapphics' of 'The Temporary the All' combine with arch diction and cumbersome alliteration to mock an idealized hope and failure of smooth achievement. But the rhythms of poems like 'Beeny Cliff' or 'The Going' are part of an exquisite music (altogether out of Meredith's tympanic range) used in conjunction with forceful dramatic revelation. Meredith uses sound effects more for imitative purposes; his rhythms approximate to the movements of natural things, establish an ambience (a march of doom or a dance of joy), or register a dramatic progress in their changes of pace.

One can easily descry in the diction of these poets equivalents of Ruskin's Gothic ornament which

     stands out in prickly independence, and frosty fortitude, jutting

into crockets, and freezing into pinnacles; here starting up into a
monster, there germinating into a blossom, anon knitting itself into
a branch, alternately thorny, bossy, and bristly, or writhed into
every form of nervous entanglement; but, even when most graceful,
never for an instant languid, always quickset: erring, if at all, ever
on the side of brusquerie.

(*SV*, II.vi.240)

Both poets savage the reader's ear with a rattle of consonants,
awkward neologisms, and frequent syntactical eccentricities
enforcing compression or emphasis. Hardy's use of such devices
almost invariably amplifies the significance of his words. His
predilection for negative forms, for instance, ranges from a simple
all-stifling monotony of 'no' or 'not', to frequent and calculated
use of the 'un-' prefix (such verbs register an objective absence
of activity and a subjective recognition of its continuing failure),
to negative forms of words whose opposite is usually some
different word ('unsight', 'Nescience', 'disennoble'). Negatives
rendered actively ('unknows', 'Nescience mutely muses'), or
quantitatively ('On which lost the more by our love'), gain force.

Meredith, like Hardy, presses diction to the service of imitation,
from simple onomatopoeic effects ('Yaffles on a chuckle skim')
to grotesque coinings often betraying the author into an imitative
fallacy ('The friable and the grumous, dizzards both'). Meredith
is skilled in painting nature's colours in words and evoking her
motions in sound. But the effects of wedding over-indulgent
imitation with explanation can be grotesque.

Yesterday's clarion cock scudded hen of the invalid comb;
They, the triumphant tonant towering upper, were under;
They, violators of home, dared hope an inviolate home;
They that had stood for the stroke were the vigorous hewers;
Quick as the trick of the wrist with the rapier, they the
    pursuers.

('The Revolution', st. x)

The ironist's double vision is inherently grotesque in its
incapacity to overlook the bleakly humorous guises a fundamental
tragedy can assume. Meredith directs this vision towards his
subjects, while awareness of his own fallibility underlies many
of Hardy's best poetic jokes. That awareness, which Hardy lets
his readers share, provokes the self-conscious, pretentious, eminently collapsible diction of 'The Temporary the All', and is

summed up in the line, 'Thus I. . . . But lo, me!' The forms of Hardy's poetry often enhance the incongruities which nature supplies. Unbelief and unhope ring out in the common metre of songs of faith. A homely deceased community announces its carelessness of the world's progress in a metre approximating to that of 'Locksley Hall'; and the graceful dactyls of 'The Voice' falter as the reality of loss supersedes the consolations of reverie. Hardy makes himself or his neighbour appear grotesque because his artistic consciousness harbours the knowledge that the antitype of caricature—the whole knowledge or the perfect record—is impossible.

Hardy made Meredith's works part of 'the vast universal volume which enshrines as contributors all those that have adequately recorded their reading of life'. The final words are Meredith's—they belong to his last volume of poetry, and state the aim of all his work. Hardy's 'vast universal volume' is the ever-incomplete record of mortal experience, of which no ideal complete record exists, or can exist, in or beyond the world. That Meredith should have contributed to it an 'adequate' record is not a dismissive phrase, for such a contribution is Hardy's own necessarily limited aim. 'Unadjusted impressions', Hardy explains, 'have their value', for 'the road to a true philosophy of life seems to lie in humbly recording diverse readings of its phenomena as they are forced upon us by chance and change' (Preface, *Poems of the Past and the Present*).

The differences with which Hardy and Meredith approach this common task are exaggerated by their authorial postures. Hardy's 'dramatic or impersonative' method displays the sign-seeker delving in subjective experience to find a principle of unity in the fugitive impressions which he has 'never tried to co-ordinate'. He is looking to learn on a cosmic level, as he did on the personal, that 'All these specimens of man, / So various in their pith and plan, / Curious to say / Were *one* man' ('So Various').

Meredith's 'philosophical' poems posit an objective view of the enduring vitality of an unquestioning nature. But his over-wrought insistence on the fairness of things underlines the gap between the reality of the phenomenal world he loves and the ideality of an understanding of its origins, meaning, or purpose. Both poets cultivate an over-simplified authorial pose to co-ordinate their vision in poetry, the optimist who has come through his 'faith's ordeal' no less than the old armadillo of 'He Never Expected Much'.

Hardy and Meredith find their world lacking a received text—scriptural, philosophic, or scientific—sufficient in itself as a reading of life. Sensitive on the one hand to the activities of 'change and chancefulness' which yield injustice and incongruity, and on the other hand, to the proposed congruities of Darwinian evolution, both adopt the natural world as their text. They con it without the aid of 'Assurances, symbols, saws, / Revelations in Legends' ('A Faith on Trial'). Hardy looks at what is 'written on terrestrial things', for analogies with men's experience; Meredith 'reads' Earth's multifarious life as a man who is part of that life, and who, understanding it, may understand himself.

Both are aware of occupying a hiatus between the naïve and the mature. In a simpler stage, of belief and faith, Hardy says, 'We could read men's dreams . . . Now we are blinker-bound' ('Yuletide in a Younger World'). Evolutionary growth brings with it the pain of outgrowing superstitions with no firm promise of mature understanding. Both beseech 'more brain' for a world which dwells in Nescience, or has misplaced its reading specs, or has only inched its way towards consciousness in the vast tracts of evolutionary time.

Meredith's 'Earth and Man' traces man's progress from 'lusty animal' to the infantile reasoner who turns from his mother earth because to 'his blank eye' her ways appear blindness (the very figure of Hardy's blind genetrix). The confused creature rails against the notion that nature cherishes her fittest members,

> Albeit thereof he has found
> Firm roadway between lustfulness and pain;
> Has half transferred the battle to his brain,
> From bloody ground.   (st. xvi)

Whereas Hardy's Earth laments such precociousness, Meredith's feels pride in her child's intellectual struggles, seeing man's evolution is part of her own development:

> Through him hath she exchanged,
> For the gold harvest-robes, the mural crown,
> Her haggard quarry-features and thick frown
> Where monsters ranged.   (st. xxvi)

Man's ironically misguided effort to rise above nature has given her new refinements of order and mind. Language is the triumph of evolution, the perfected vehicle for the examination and expression of the phenomenal world, and the means of reading the permanence of man's place in the natural continuity ('. . . a land / Whereon his labour is a carven page; / And forth from heritage to heritage / Nought writ on sand', st. xxxix). The 'word' is traditionally the meeting-place of the noumenal and the phenomenal. Meredith images the language-acquirer himself as Nature's 'great word of life' (st. xliv), making him thus her 'chief expression' and earnest of purposefulness. The reader and the text meet in man.

What define Meredith's optimism and Hardy's 'pessimism' are Meredith's confidence that earth *can* be read and Hardy's dismay that man's evolved consciousness serves only to discover the wrongness of things. Hardy tries various sleights to get round his own 'limitings' or the intransigent obscurity of the real to reach 'the Back of Things'. He personifies a perfected human consciousness in those who have passed from life and in the Spirits of *The Dynasts*, only to recognize that such a view registered in art can see no further than the informing intelligence of the work's author. Whereas Meredith links the real and ideal in man as word, Hardy's failure to link them is registered in the absence of words, from his reticence when confronted by the puzzles of nature's questioning ('No answerer I') to the ironic silence of 'He Resolves to Say No More'. The integrity of Hardy's failure is registered when he admits his preference for the real over possible idealist escape-routes. The pain of unknowing *and* the love of the real which spurs Hardy's compassionate search for the better are characteristically present in the concluding lines of 'He Prefers Her Earthly' (442):

> I would not have you thus and there,
> But still would grieve on, missing you, still feature
> You as the one you were.

Hardy's idea that there is no ruling plan makes any individual's vision necessarily subjective, and locates the essence of poetry in that subjectivity: 'The poetry of a scene varies with the minds of the perceivers. Indeed, it does not lie in the scene at all' (*Life*, p. 50). For this reason external nature in Hardy's poetry links a speaker to his past, or participates in or reflects the sorrows and joys known to men. Hardy often directs attention to the seer to show that the only 'law' of nature is the subjectivity of her creatures. This is the burden of 'The King's Experiment' and many others, and it influences the techniques as well as the subjects of Hardy's poetry.

The subjective view and its capacity to undermine the poet's reading are humorously illustrated in 'The Milkmaid'. The poet idealizes and misreads his pastoral 'Phyllis', who does not commune with nature, but indulges selfish, mundane thoughts. While thus mocking his own 'poetic' expectations, the observer recognizes the girl's thoughts as the shapers of consciousness, the only operative point of contact with reality, as the 'inner themes and inner poetries'.

'In Front of the Landscape' presents a more sober experience of subjectivity and of the observed world's indecipherability. Here the poet's consciousness fills with visions of the past, obscuring the visible landscape. A complex irony grips the poem when the poet adopts the eyes of outer reality—'passing people'—to see himself as one who walks 'seeing nought / Round him that looms / Whithersoever his footsteps turn in his farings, / Save a few tombs'. Subjectivity, which prevents his seeing the landscape, makes others blind to his inner themes. But the persistence of those themes in obscuring the present reality—a preoccupation with the past has been exchanged for his former preoccupation with the future—signals a continuing loss to the poet and lends an ironic validity to the seemingly limited image of the self-absorbed poet as a man 'seeing nought'.

Hardy's mirror technique and his solipsism invariably place him in front of a landscape which, though he may wander a lifetime over its face, is only partially seen, admits no penetration 'behind', and only throws back a reflection of the perceiver. An effort to 'read' such a landscape is a cruel joke. It is the intolerable irony which lodges at the heart of Hardy's most ambitious poetical effort, *The Dynasts*.

The joke is allowed to *be* one in 'The Milestone by the Rabbit-Burrow' where the rabbit, who tries to guess the writing on the milestone by reading the expressions of the passers-by, falls victim to the pathetic fallacy and interprets the stone's significance in terms of rabbithood.

Hardy makes the pathetic fallacy a means to communication when 'reading' and 'reason' fail. Such a failure of reading in 'The Darkling Thrush', finds the poet trapped in a universal mirror of his mood, seeing no cause for ecstatic sound 'written on terrestrial things / Afar or nigh around'. Hardy reaches beyond his own mood to find a meaning for the thrush's song through a reversal of the pathetic fallacy, attributing joy, happiness, and a hope to the sound which refuses to fit his hopeless inner themes and poetries. Feeling thus shows the poet his 'limitings' *and* his participation in an existence of wider consciousness.

'The Wind Blew Words' justifies the pathetic technique as a means to such participation. The wind's 'words' provide a text for the aspiring consciousness through the pathetic fallacy. ('Behold this troubled tree, / Complaining as it sways and plies; / It is a limb of thee'.) They teach the poet his kinship with vegetable, animal, and the various human creation, enabling him to see the whole as a 'pathetic ME'. He has gone beyond projecting his feelings onto nature; he has projected all the deaths, breakages, or thwartings seen in nature onto himself, whereupon *in him* they become felt. It is a masterful poetic reversal and labels the pathetic fallacy as a meeting place for 'inner themes' and life at large.

Meredith reaches sympathy with nature through a different kind of involvement; although he animates and personifies, he restrains the pathetic technique and only occasionally allows his nature to verbalize. Meredith's wind does not blow words. It blows the trees, the clouds, the grass. His favourite wind, the South-Wester, is beloved for its pure energy which, girding itself in atmospheric colour and calling forth sounds in its relationship to physical nature, seems to embody itself.

> For lo, beneath those ragged clouds
> That skirt the opening west, a stream
> Of yellow light and windy flame
> Spreads lengthening southward, and the sky
> Begins to gloom, and o'er the ground
> A moan of coming blasts creeps low
> And rustles in the crisping grass;
> Till suddenly with mighty arms
> Outspread, that reach the horizon round,

The great South-West drives o'er the earth
And loosens all his roaring robes
Behind him, over heath and moor.

('South-West Wind in the Woodland')

Its effects suggest a multitude of personified forms to the poet. Meredith allows his imagination to play over the suggestive sights and sounds accompanying the South-Wester's passage, and in a proliferation of similes the wind becomes a force involving disparate nature: '. . . like an eagle's wing . . . a sail that tacks . . . an anguish'd thing . . . a breaking heart . . . a storm-charged cloud . . . a woodland dove'. Meredith's sympathy is based in the knowledge that 'every elemental power / Is kindred to our hearts, and once / Acknowledged, wedded, once embraced, / . . . The union is eternal.' Nor does this intimation of immortality in nature blind him to a shared mortality. This he accepts too, without question.

The pine-tree drops its dead;
They are quiet, as under the sea.
Overhead, overhead
Rushes life in a race,
As the clouds the clouds chase;
    And we go,
And we drop like the fruits of the tree,
    Even we,
    Even so.

('Dirge in Woods')

Hardy sympathizes with nature by assimilating its life to his being—creating 'a pathetic ME'; Meredith assimilates his life to nature's being in which he finds a true, as opposed to a sentimental, sympathy. These differences of approach colour the 'words' that nature offers its two readers. Although he has abandoned the old god to see by the light of science, Hardy would like to find in nature words to replace revelation. Natural selection, neither just nor compassionate, suggests a thwarted purposing, or worse, an unfeeling one. Nature exhibits only fellow-sufferers and questioners ('We wonder, ever wonder, Why we find us here!') or a fellow-cynic, rejecting the possibility that

'Life is for ends unknown':

> It says that Life would signify
>   A thwarted purposing:
> That we come to live, and are called to die.
>   Yes, that's the thing
>   In fall, in spring,
>   That Yell'ham says:—
>   'Life offers—to deny!'
>   ('Yell'ham-Wood's Story')

Meredith's woodland says,

> We brood, we strive to sky,
> We gaze upon decay,
> We wot of life through death,
> How each feeds each we spy;
> And is a tangle round,
> Are patient; what is dumb
> We question not, nor ask
> The silent to give sound,
> The hidden to unmask,
> The distant to draw near.
>   ('Woodland Peace')

When he looks to earth the poet finds that 'nothing of love it said' ('In the Woods'). Earth can neither ask nor answer questions of love, justice, 'hope or fear', the why or the 'whence'. It can merely continually develop. In this Meredith finds ground for optimism and a lesson of acceptance.

> I know not hope or fear;
> I take whate'er may come;
> I raise my head to aspects fair,
> From foul I turn away.

This is not, as generally misread, *Meredith*'s statement of personal optimism; it is the *woodland*'s announcement of an evolutionary pursuit of perfection. Meredith's optimism rests in his reconciliation to mortality and local chance in acceptance of a process greater than the offering or denial of individual lives.

Hardy and Meredith extended their readings to human nature as recorded in history's text, Hardy in *The Dynasts*, Meredith notably in his *Odes in Contribution to the Song of French History*[9] and 'The Nuptials of Attila'. Both discovered in the history of empires *exempla* of the local grandeur and general insignificance of man. Each embodies his vision in characteristically Gothic forms, notably symmetry of structure (in dramatic progress and development of argument); a calculated use of 'ornamentation' to highlight or give shape to a fundamental mass of observed 'fact'; the use of nature as a literal and metaphorical element in a work of art whose subject is human experience; a perspective within the work blending distant overview and precisely observed detail to link the particular with the general; and a sense / intelligence dichotomy which presents a problem and a possibility rather than a solution.

'Flat as to an eagle's eye, / Earth hung under Attila.' The opening perspective of 'The Nuptials of Attila' suggests the bird's-eye view of Hardy's dumb shows (which is also familiar in his fiction). A generalized view of the lives of men who 'wax again, / Crawl, and in their manner die' anticipates Hardy's more detailed reverse-telescope scenes which repeatedly reduce humanity to insect proportions: 'a file of ants crawling along a strip of garden-matting . . . .'[10]

In assuming an 'overworld' point of view, both Hardy and Meredith make use of personification to emphasize the organic entity which is the people of a nation or a continent. Hardy's Europe 'is disclosed as a prone and emaciated figure, the Alps shaping like a backbone, and the branching mountain-chains like ribs, the peninsular plateau of Spain forming a head' (p. 27). Meredith's pre-Revolutionary France is introduced in 'The Revolution' with 'And low the Gallic Giantess lay enchained . . . .'

The point of view which 'sinks downwards through space, and draws near to the surface of the perturbed countries' in Hardy's opening vision, to see 'the peoples . . . in their various cities and nationalities' (p. 27), and ultimately to focus on individuals, has its analogue in the descent in 'Alsace-Lorraine' (st. iii) from general overview (a personified France) to surface activity (her people 'by the serious looms, / Afield, in factories, with the birds astir . . .'), to its particular components ('the thought . . . spoken sometimes in low tone / At lip or in a fluttered look').

In the absence of motion a distantly-viewed scene can assume the character of an artefact. Attila's host in inactivity appears as a stone statue, 'Like the charger cut in stone . . . .' To Hardy's bird's-eye view, the Iberian peninsula 'features itself somewhat like a late-Gothic shield . . . .' Here, as in his personification of Spain, Hardy's figure organizes a wide field of vision, giving it unity, and the activities within it a character. Meredith's use of the artefact analogy, like his personifications, has the effect of expanding significance, serving as a metaphor for the condition of a whole society, or clue to the character and fate of a people.

Hardy's Napoleon is the writer of a destined story: 'History makes use of me to weave her web / To her long while aforetime-figured mesh / And contemplated charactery' (p. 449). For a moment the brain-like composite creature of the dumb shows seems animated by his life, but the brevity of the moment signals its insignificance. 'Great men are meteors that consume themselves / To light the earth. This is my burnt-out hour' (p. 700). The Spirit of the Years labels him a servant of necessity.

> Such men . . .
> Are in the elemental ages' chart
> Like meanest insects on obscurest leaves
> But incidents and grooves of Earth's unfolding;
> Or as the brazen rod that stirs the fire
> Because it must.

Only Napoleon's awareness that he is an agent of an unseen Will affords him heroism in Hardy's scheme. Meredith's Napoleon, servant of a destiny he shares with France, is preeminently a servant of Self. Meredith pits the would-be god against 'those firm laws / Which we name Gods' ('France, December, 1870', st. vii): change and continuity (the laws which defeat Attila's dynastic dream). The common view in 'Napoléon' reveals an illusion the egoist shares with men at large: 'Who looked on him beheld the will of wills' (Hardy's Spirit of the Years could indulge a grim grin), sustained by ignorance 'And he, the reader of men, himself unread . . . .' Yet Meredith's titan, too, is 'The Necessitated'. However much he exceeds 'heroical Romance' or 'ensanguined History's lengthened scroll', he is only a part of the self-writing story of Earth. This truth mocks the egoist's own deluded pose as a writer (Meredith, too, summons meteoric light):

> From off the meteor gleam of his waved sword
> Reflected bright in permanence: she bled
> As the Bacchante spills her challengeing wine
> With whirl o' the cup before the kiss to lip;

And bade drudge History in his footprints tread,
For pride of sword-strokes o'er slow penmanship:
Each step of his a volume: his sharp word
The shower of steel and lead
Or pastoral sunshine.

(st. iv)

Hardy places Napoleon by viewing the absorption of the figure into the carpet, 'but one flimsy riband of Its web'. Meredith exposes the egoist's limitations by enabling France herself to read the tyrant by comparison with her 'heavenly lover', Liberty, and with herself: 'Mannerless, graceless, laughterless, unlike / Herself in all . . . / Partly she read her riddle, stricken and pained' (st. x). Reading her tyrant rightly, France resigns 'the shell of that much limited man' to its mortal destiny, completing the self-doom of the misreader:

By the hands that built him up was he undone:
. . .
By his own force, the suicide in his mill.
Needs never God of Vengeance intervene
When giants their last lesson have to learn.

(st. xiii)

The end of *The Dynasts*, where Hardy's Napoleon rehearses his might-have-been, is above anything Meredith could do in prose or verse by virtue of its stark, precisely simple visual setting and its multiple ironies. The solitary, spent figure self-communing in the moonlight is near-tragic. But his solitariness is ironically tinged by the overworld perspective. The Emperor who announces his 'lurid loneliness' is not alone. He is privy to the musings of the Spirits and he remains an undifferentiated part of the Will he has 'passively obeyed'. To the last he sees his fate in terms of power, but his powerlessness is highlighted by the very life which, even in the midst of his death-dealing, has refused to relinquish him betimes.

Both poets enquire of Nature's continuity and changefulness its value. Meredith sees evolution as improvement, however halting, and he associates education with the process. In the France odes, the cycles of abasement and triumph, slavery and liberation spiral into an evolutionary progress towards 'light'. When the 'vessel' which was his Napoleon has sunk in the storm of battle and the waves of Time, the image of the 'treasure-galleon' which was his ideal of liberty persists. Though Hardy's confidence in the equation of evolution and improvement was to wane with time, *The Dynasts*, the last of his works written and published in Meredith's lifetime, harbours amidst its ironies a vision of such evolution. The Spirit of the Years calls the fates of greatest men 'But incidents and grooves of Earth's unfolding'. Huxley's explanation of evolution, quoted by Hardy's friend Clodd in his *Animism* (1905), emphasized the multiplication of cerebral grooves as the sign of progressive evolutionary development. Hardy's image suggests that the brain-web organism of the overworld view may harbour a purpose. The Spirit of the Pities poses that as a part has evolved cognition, so might the whole, and this is the single argument of the Compassionates that the Spirit of the Years must admit, for he, too, has evolved in understanding from the dreaming stage ('Yea, I psalmed thus and thus') to the empirical (the sense of what is 'consistent with our spectacle', p. 705) and the rational ('so far as reasonings tell', p. 702). The insistent questionings of the semichoruses signal a continuing search for understanding (a dream of a Will righting suffering and injustice 'In a genial germing purpose, and for loving-kindness' sake': p. 706), and even more than the concluding dart of optimism, manifest Hardy's evolutionary meliorism.

Deeply embedded in *The Dynasts* and ever-present to the poet who wrote *Modern Love* is that sense of imperfection which Ruskin found essential to the nature of Gothic. Hardy's art challenges its own limits in a bold heterogeneity of realism and stylization, earnestness and mockery. It boasts fidelity to nature in its minutely observed rendering of life, while never disguising its designer's vision. Meredith's work does not bring alive in homely particularity the 'vast various moils that mean a world alive', but uses exaggerated simplification, in personification, allegory and metaphor, to wed nature's facts and the artist's fancy in an idiosyncratic reading of life. Language for both poets holds the promise of harmony and the example of painful discord. Meredith's words, likening life to art, speak for their common effort.

> But listen in the thought; so may there come
> Conception of a newly-added chord,
> Commanding space beyond where ear has home.

In labour of the trouble at its fount,
Leads Life to an intelligible Lord
The rebel discords up the sacred mount.

                    ('The Promise in Disturbance')

NOTES

1. C. L. Cline, ed., *The Letters of George Meredith* (Oxford 1970), i, 431.
2. 'G. M.: A Reminiscence', reprinted in Harold Orel, ed., *Thomas Hardy's Personal Writings* (1967), p. 152. (Hereafter *PW*)
3. Meredith 'spoke (needlessly) in favour of his continuing', but wished it were in prose, 'where he is more at home than in verse, though here and there he produces good stuff', *Letters*, iii, 1530.
4. J. O. Bailey, *The Poetry of Thomas Hardy: A Handbook and Commentary* (Chapel Hill, 1970), p. 259.
5. D. H. Lawrence, *The English Review* 9 (1911), 723.
6. Phyllis B. Bartlett, ed., *The Poems of George Meredith* (New Haven, 1978), i. 143. All quotations are from this edition; printing errors have been emended.
7. John Ruskin, *The Stones of Venice*, II, vi, 190, in E. T. Cook and Alexander Wedderburn, eds., *The Works of John Ruskin* (1903–12), vol. x. (Hereafter *SV*)
8. [George Meredith], *The Westminster Review*, n.s. 12 (July 1857), 314.
9. *Odes in Contribution to the Song of French History* (1898), included 'France, December 1870' (originally published 1871), *Poems*, i, 369–79, 'The Revolution', *Poems*, i, 553–64, 'Napoléon', *Poems*, i, 564–90, 'Alsace-Lorraine', *Poems*, i, 591–610.
10. *The Dynasts*, ed. Harold Orel (1978), p. 379.

7

Hardy's Inconsistent Spirits and the Philosophic Form of *The Dynasts*

by G. GLEN WICKENS

'The real offence of *The Dynasts*', Hardy said, 'lies, not in its form as such, but in the philosophy which gave rise to the form'.[1] His remark focuses attention not merely on the exasperating objections of contemporary reviewers to a 'philosophy which has never been expressed in poetry before' (*Life*, p. 319), but also on the unequivocal demand *The Dynasts* makes to be read as a philosophic poem. By dividing his epic into a human world and an Overworld, Hardy created a philosophic form, and his poem cannot be evaluated without consideration of its large controlling ideas.

Hardy created his Overworld to replace the 'old theologies' of the Greek, Roman, and Christian epics, but he did not see his poem as a consistent argument, 'since, like *Paradise Lost, The Dynasts* proves nothing' (*Life*, pp. 319, 454). His cosmic Spectators are, as they say themselves and as he said more than once, 'but the flower of Man's intelligence',[2] no more than 'the best human intelligences of their time in a sort of quint-essential form' (*Life*, p. 321). All of Hardy's Intelligences, including the Spirit of the Years, are, by his own testimony, inconsistent, but their inconsistency reflects the imperfections of contemporary thought. To understand the function of the two main philosophic Voices in the poem, the Spirit of the Pities and the Spirit of the Years, we need to understand Hardy's use of the contradictions he found in the scientific and philosophic thought of his age, and rather than dismissing his Overworld because of its inconsistency, we can, more profitably, examine his design.

Hardy's portrayal of the Spirit of the Years in Part I of *The*

Dynasts recalls the official position of many scientists and materialist philosophers at the start of the post-Darwinian period.
The oldest Voice of the nineteenth century confidently describes
a deterministic cosmos of fixed and knowable laws and proclaims
that the Immanent Will operates like a vast machine: the 'Prime
Mover of the year', it says (Fore Scene, p. 6), reduces the peoples
of Europe to 'flesh-hinged mannikins Its Hand upwinds / To
click-clack off Its preadjusted laws' (Fore Scene, p. 4). But behind
this extreme Voice of scientific rationalism is Hardy's awareness
of the steady movement of nineteenth-century science and philosophy towards a complete synthesis of man and nature. The
'prevailing reductionist naturalism'[3] which followed widespread
acceptance of Darwin's theory of evolution had such an impact
on him that he wrote *The Dynasts* to counter the belief that
science, and its master key, natural selection, could solve the
riddle of the universe and reconcile all contradictions. The cosmic
perspective of the Spirit of the Years, then, is certainly not the
'philosophy' of the poem. It is manipulated as an aspect of truth,
not presented as a wholly truthful argument. Hardy uses it to
set up a challenge which the rest of the poem, and especially the
Voice of Pity, seeks to meet, not by evading the facts of science
and the analysis of pessimism, but by reinterpreting them into
a sacramental vision of the Will which can at once objectively
describe phenomena and affirm the validity of the subjective and
spiritual response of man the observer.

Hardy's 'imaginative solace' (*Life*, p. 310), the idealism which
he opposes to the reductionist naturalism of the Spirit of the
Years, is, like his Will, groping and tentative. He makes it more
than merely a flimsy thread in the poem's pattern by undermining
the deterministic cosmology. The Spirit of the Years contradicts
itself in its account of man's relation to the Will: 'ITS slaves we
are: ITS slaves must ever be!' it says (First, VI, viii, p. 137), but
Hardy works by implication to strengthen the idea of the difference between the human will and the Immanent Will. Commenting on the revolt of the Prussian people against Napoleon,
the Voice of determinism says:

> So doth the Will objectify Itself
> In likeness of a sturdy people's wrath,
> Which takes no count of the new trends of time,
> Trusting ebbed glory in a present need.—

What if their strength should equal not their fire,
And their devotion dull their vigilance?—
Uncertainly, by fits the Will doth work
In Brunswick's blood, their chief as in themselves;
It ramifies in streams that intermit
And make their movement vague, old fashioned, slow
To foil the modern methods counterposed!
(Second, I, iii, pp. 155–56)

The nouns 'wrath', 'fire', 'blood', and the verb 'intermit', associated with fever, point to a Will that works through instinctive
emotion and blind passion. The implied criticism, and one that
cannot escape the reader despite the speaker, depends on the
contrast between 'vigilance' and unconsciousness. On two other
occasions, the Spirit of the Years supports the idea that man can
and should resist the irrational forces of nature. In its comments
on the 'wholesale butchery' at Borodino (Third, I, vi, p. 344),
this cosmic Spectator indicates that man is linked to the weaving
Will chiefly through the survival instincts of the species, and the
same dualistic view of nature versus human nature is unmistak-
ably present in the Spirit of the Years' observation near the end
of the battle of Waterloo,

. . . that all wide sight and self-command
Desert these throngs now driven to demonry
By the Immanent Unrecking. Naught remains
But the vindictiveness here amid the strong,
And there amid the weak an impotent rage.
(Third, VII, viii, p. 517)

By focusing on the soldiers' loss of foresight and moral control,
the Voice of the Years intimates that conscious man's freedom
from the 'Unrecking' lies in his ability to assert the distinctly
human qualities of reason and ethical fellow-feeling and to arrest
the Darwinian struggle for existence.

Even in the detached, intellectual stance of the Spirit of the
Years, Hardy sounds, although faintly, one of the main optimistic
notes of his epic-drama, the belief that unconscious force will not
always reduce history to a continuous trail of blood. At the same
time, what remains implicit in the Voice of the Years becomes
explicit in the Voice of Pity: 'They are shapes that bleed, mere
mannikins or no, / And each has parcel in the total Will' (Fore

Scene, p. 4). In the Fore Scene, the Chorus of Pities clearly outlines to the Shade of the Earth who the ideal leaders should be:

> We would establish those of kindlier build,
>   In fair Compassions skilled,
> Men of deep art in life-development;
> Watchers and warders of thy varied lands,
>   Men surfeited of laying heavy hands
>   Upon the innocent,
> The mild, the fragile, the obscure content
> Among the myriads of thy family.
> Those, too, who love the true, the excellent,
> And make their daily moves a melody.   (p. 3)

The sympathetic Intelligence constantly expresses the need for an ethic of loving-kindness which Hardy felt not only as part of his Christian background but also as the great fact indicated by the monistic and evolutionary idea of nature. The centre of altruism must be shifted first to humanity as a whole, then to all of suffering, sentient life which, Christ-like, 'shoulders its cross anew' (Second, VI, vii, p. 321). Those leaders at the forefront of evolution, whose 'art' of ethical awareness and sensitivity is most highly developed, must act as the shepherd to his flock, the gardener to his garden, cultivating a civilization in continuity and harmony with the 'innocent' part of creation.

While at times showing sympathy for various military leaders and dynasts, including Napoleon after Waterloo, the Spirit of the Pities is mainly concerned with the peoples of Europe 'enmeshed in new calamity' (Second, I, viii, p. 180), as they form a compact, suffering whole. After Napoleon's overthrow in 1814, the idealistic Spirit believes that it is

> . . . but Napoléon who has failed.
> The pale pathetic peoples still plod on
> Through hoodwinkings to light!
>   (Third, IV, iv, p. 414)

It desires an increased political freedom, presumably along democratic lines, but a freedom that can be meaningful only in terms of an ethical vision which makes no nationalistic distinctions. Nationalism may be necessary to help bring about Napoleon's defeat, but in the total picture of an evolving nature with man at the conscious head, such blind patriotism is only another symptom of Europe's great problem, of man's relapse into the spontaneous course of nature's Will.

Hardy knew there were some serious problems with the Spirit of the Pities' ideal of the ethical will directing the amoral Will, no matter how many scientists and philosophers supported such a distinction despite their monistic assumptions about nature. In the first place, man is, to some extent, placed in an adversary relationship with the Will: he struggles against his own instinctive being and wars with nature outside himself, creating potentially tragic divisions. In the second place, scientists like Huxley realistically undermined the ultimate goal of the entire moral and civilized effort and with apocalyptic gloom predicted that 'man may develop a worthy civilization ... until the evolution of our globe shall have entered so far upon its downward course that the cosmic process resumes its sway; and, once more, the State of Nature prevails over the surface of our planet'.[4]

Hardy could not let the meliorism of *The Dynasts* rest with man alone; he had to redeem, at least partially, the bleak facts of Darwin's nature and to place the hope for man's moral development, his use of right reason, in a much wider evolutionary context of affirmation. Significantly, some of the unanalyzed assumptions of scientists themselves gave Hardy the option of seeing purpose as well as process in evolution. He could manipulate, for example, the anthropomorphic interpretation of the physical order which, for all their claims to empirical objectivity, the exponents of natural knowledge continued to use. The Spirit of the Years' metaphor, 'And mark the game now played there by the Master-hand!' (Second, II, iii, p. 196), suggests that the Will has some intention in the same way that Darwin's metaphors transform natural selection into an immanent and omniscient God dictating the progression of all life, 'daily and hourly scrutinizing, throughout the world, every variation, even the slightest, rejecting that which is bad, preserving and adding up all that is good'.[5]

By having the Voice of the Years refer to the Will as a master chess player, Hardy also plays with the juridical respect of many scientists for the laws of nature. Huxley says that 'The chessboard is the world, the pieces are the phenomena of the universe, the rules of the game are what we call the laws of nature', and, similarly, John Tyndall writes of 'the methods by which the physical universe is ordered and ruled'.[6] Hardy takes the idea of purpose implicit in the metaphor of the prescriptive rule of law and makes the Spirit of the Years imply a view of the Immanent Will that goes beyond scientific description. Even when speaking most officially, the Voice of the Years adds a new dimension to the Will: 'You cannot swerve the pulsion of the Byss, / Which thinking on, yet weighing not Its thought, / Unchecks Its clock-like laws.' The Will may appear to work mindlessly through the precision of mechanical laws but It 'thinks' in some way nevertheless. 'It works unconsciously, as heretofore, / Eternal artistries in Circumstance' (Fore Scene, p. 1), yet as an artist It must have some kind of aim. In an important passage, Hardy has the Spirit of the Years define this aim in terms of unconscious planning:

> In that immense unweeting Mind is shown
> One far above forethinking; processive,
> Rapt, superconscious; a Clairvoyancy
> That knows not what It knows, yet works therewith.
>
> (First, V, iv, p. 99)

The exposition of the Will here passes openly into metaphysics and shows the influence of Eduard von Hartmann's *The Philosophy of the Unconscious*. In his 'Literary Notes II', Hardy paraphrased a number of passages from Hartmann, including his definition of the Unconscious as the 'united unconscious will & unconscious idea', and his paradoxical idea of 'unconscious thinking'.[7] It is only necessary to glance at Hartmann's prefaces to understand why Hardy must have read the *Philosophy of the Unconscious* with as much interest and care as he obviously did the *Origin of Species*. Hartmann describes his aim as to produce 'an idealistic philosophy beside and above the mechanical cosmic theory of the Sciences of Matter'.[8] He says that 'It is my firm conviction that the exclusively mechanical Cosmism of Darwinism is only an historical transition from the prior shallow materialism to a complete and whole Ideal-realism' (*PU*, I, xxv). His whole philosophy is an attempt to comprehend and unify the facts of science and the wisdom of intuition, 'to pour a mystical conception into an adequately scientific mould' (*PU*, I, 10). Aware that 'in every department of life Realism is triumphant over Idealism' (*PU*, I, 11), he tries to redress the balance and to act as a spokesman for both inductive evidence and those speculative principles which are 'mystically gained' (*PU*, I, 13).

What Hardy could not have missed in the *Philosophy of the .Unconscious* was a significant philosophic equivalent of his own lifelong attempt to 'reconcile a scientific view of life with the emotional and spiritual' (*Life*, p. 148). Hartmann argues that the 'concept "mechanism" does not exhaust the facts' (*PU*, I, 199) and wants to transcend the prevalent image of nature as a machine: 'Thus every organism is comparable to a steam-engine; it is, however, also at the same time stoker and engine-driver, nay, repairer also, and . . . even its own fabricator' (*PU*, I, 172). Whereas Darwin cannot explain how the machine made itself, Hartmann tries to make plausible 'the validity of the assumption of an Aim in Nature' (*PU*, I, 43) through the purposive activity of the Unconscious Will. Much like Hardy himself, he speaks of man's 'repugnance to the thought, in default of a conscious God, of being a product of blind natural forces, unintended, unwatched, purposeless and transient result of a fortuitous necessity' (*PU*, II, 245–46). To find a substitute for God, he proposes 'an ideal formative impulse of the Unconscious' (*PU*, II, 120) that unerringly directs evolution to a great cosmic end. The Unconscious acts as an immanent providence that leads the human race in the direction of sympathy and altruism and away from individual selfish impulses. Unlike Huxley, Hartmann ultimately brings man's social and ethical development into harmony with the cosmic process. The supreme ethical principle becomes: '*TO MAKE THE ENDS OF THE UNCONSCIOUS ENDS OF OUR CONSCIOUSNESS*' (*PU*, III, 133). Hartmann thus restores man to a sacramental relationship with God. The civilized consciousness can help fulfill the purpose of the Unconscious Deity and it is this ideal that Hardy uses as the central religious hope of *The Dynasts*.

In a 'real conversation' with William Archer in 1901, Hardy, commenting on the incompleteness of alleged manifestations of a spirit world, explained how *The Philosophy of the Unconscious* helped him to speculate on a very different cosmic process from the evolutionary universe of science:

> Is not this incompleteness a characteristic of all phenomena, of the universe at large? It often seems to me like a half-expressed, an

ill-expressed idea. Do you know Hartmann's Philosophy of the Unconscious? It suggested to me what seems like a workable theory of the great problem of the origin of evil,—though this, of course, is not Hartmann's own theory,—that there may be a consciousness infinitely far off, at the other end of the chain of phenomena, always striving to express itself, and always baffled and blundering, just as the spirits seem to be.[9]

Hardy's emphasis here is on the reunion of the Idea with nature, on the world, to alter Schopenhauer, as an 'ill-expressed idea'. Using Hartmann's metaphysic as a starting point, he proceeded to formulate his own conception of the growing consciousness of the Immanent Will in contrast to Hartmann's belief that 'the will itself can never become conscious, because it can never contradict itself' (*PU*, II, 96). Both *The Philosophy of the Unconscious* and *The Dynasts* are cosmic dramas of redemption: in Hartmann the salvation of the world process, the redemption of God, rests with the collective pessimistic consciousness of humanity, itself foreseen by the Unconscious, which might one day be able to annihilate the Will and fulfill the purpose of evolution; while in Hardy, the salvation of man and nature lies both in the possibility of a growing ethical awareness in humanity as a whole and in the religious ideal that man's struggle is part of the planned development of a conscious creativity in the Immanent Will which contains man.

Like Hartmann, Hardy did speculate on a 'fundamental ultimate Wisdom at the back of things' (*Life*, p. 368) and wrote *The Dynasts* with this idea as one possible interpretation, among several, of the cosmic process. His departure from Hartmann's theories was his 'view of the unconscious force as gradually *becoming* conscious' and Hardy was right in claiming that this idea 'had never (so far as I know) been advanced before *The Dynasts* appeared' (*Life*, p. 449). The converging lines of awareness in the human mind and the Universal Mind are intimately bound together, not only in terms of man's conscious influence on his part of the Will, but also as a total expression of cosmic purpose. Hardy's final vision is of the will in man and the will in nature working harmoniously together, 'Consciousness the Will informing, till It fashion all things fair' (After Scene, p. 525). This climactic outlook on the future is the closest he came to reconciling man with that God for which, he said in 1890, 'I have been looking for . . . 50 years' (*Life*, p. 224). The conclusion is entirely fitting because *The Dynasts* is, in a way, the expression of Hardy's desire, which he recorded in 1898, to 'Write a prayer, or hymn, to One not omnipotent, but hampered; striving for our good, but unable to achieve it except occasionally' (*Life*, p. 525). 'This idea of a limited God of goodness,' as Florence Hardy says, was 'often dwelt on by Hardy' (*Life*, p. 297).

The carefully constructed order and meaning of the poem's last line is meant to convey a new harmony between man and God through evolution. By placing 'Consciousness' before 'Will', Hardy emphasizes the dramatic reversal in evolution, the ascension of conscious mind to its providential place in a nature which is both Will and Idea. The line moves to a new 'It' which will 'fashion all things fair!' The Will is now 'informed' or guided and instructed by human reason, man's ethical and rational awareness, and also 'informed' or imbued as a whole with the principle of consciousness, the Unconscious Idea raised to the level It has already reached in man. This latter meaning is the crux of the Chorus of the Pities' hope: 'Men gained cognition with the flux of time, / And wherefore not the Force informing them . . .?' (After Scene, p. 522).

Given the weight of evidence behind the scientific view of causal determinism in his day, Hardy needed Hartmann's philosophy to give poetic expression to a genuine struggle of ideas, a cosmic *drama* in which the real and the ideal, mechanism and teleology, might be brought into some kind of tentative harmony. Surely the Spirit of the Years' predominant image of the Will as a cosmic Brain, visualized five times in the poem, suggests just this very possibility. At its bleakest, the Phantom of the Years describes a cosmic Body which—in contrast to Milton's Holy Spirit which 'Dove-like satst brooding on the vast abyss'—

> heaves through Space and moulds the times,
> With mortals for Its fingers! We shall see
> Again men's passions, virtues, visions, crimes,
>> Obey resistlessly
> The mutative, unmotivated, dominant Thing
> Which sways in brooding dark their wayfaring!
>> (Second, II, ii, p. 191)

Logically, the 'brooding' body requires a head and so to explain the prime volitions of the Immanent Will the eldest Spirit also

says, 'Their sum is like the lobule of a Brain / Evolving always
that it wots not of; / A Brain whose whole connotes the Every-
where' (Fore Scene, p. 7). The word 'sum' emphasizes the idea
of a mathematically precise universe running like a clock, but
the image of the Brain organically links consciousness to the Idea
in nature. The inconsistent Voice of science can rebuke the Spirit
of the Pities' remark that human cognizance came 'unneeded /
In the economy of vitality':

> Nay, nay, nay;
> Your hasty judgments stay,
> Until the topmost cyme
> Have crowned the last entablature of Time.
> O heap not blame on that in-brooding Will.
>
> O pause, till all things all their days fulfill!
> (First, V, v, p. 100)

If the Will, 'Whose Brain perchance is Space, whose thought its
laws' (Fore Scene, p. 7), is 'brooding', Its Ideas or Laws could
change, just as humanity could be growing in ethical awareness
to help shape a world in which men act as one body, responsible
for the sufferings of others, though a world which no person in
the poem can yet grasp or foresee. By having the Spirit of the
Years explain the operation of the Will in terms of thinking,
Hardy brings back more than a hint of the kind of teleology
which Darwin's *scientific* hypothesis flatly rejected. Though
hindered and limited, the cosmic Brain may be directing evolution
towards an ultimate goal, and once this ideal is entertained the
poem's final vision of an awakening Will and the dominion of
consciousness becomes, if not more plausible, at least artistically
coherent. At the very beginning of the poem Hardy has the Spirit
of the Years outline three possible interpretations of the problem
of evil, two of which stress the misuse of consciousness, human
and cosmic. 'As one sad story runs,' the fault lies with a Will
capable of directing human affairs, and from this idea the Spirit
of the Pities hopes 'that though Its consciousness / May be
estranged, engrossed afar, or sealed, / Sublunar shocks may wake
Its watch anon?' But, continues the Spirit of the Years,

> Some, too, have told at whiles that rightfully
> Its warefulness, Its care, this planet lost

When in her early growth and crudity
By mad acts of severance men contrived,
Working such nescience by their own device.
(Fore Scene, p. 2)

Both these interpretations of the origin of evil, the 'great problem' of which Hardy found a 'workable theory' in Hartmann's *The Philosophy of the Unconscious*, recognize the significance of ethical purpose in evolution. The deterministic Voice of the Years rejects the idea of responsibility, of course, and provides a third alternative:

In the Foretime, even to the germ of Being,
Nothing appears of shape to indicate
That cognizance has marshalled things terrene,
Or will (such is my thinking) in my span.
(Fore Scene, p. 2)

Obviously no human type of consciousness has constructed a world characterized by the struggle for existence, but this does not rule out the possibility of some kind of unconscious or imperfect Intelligence which could one day join forces with human consciousness to fashion the world with purpose. The metaphor which the Spirit of the Years uses to explain the idea of purposeless evolution is significant. Like 'a knitter drowsed, / Whose fingers play in skilled unmindfulness' the Will has woven a great Darwinian web of life 'with an absent heed / Since life first was' and 'ever will so weave' (Fore Scene, p. 2). Again, the metaphor does not perfectly describe a cosmic process which works accidentally, but instead contains the kind of paradoxical idea which Hartmann uses to convey the purpose of an Unconscious Intelligence in nature. The point is that despite the Spirit of the Years' professed attitude toward evolution, Hardy leaves the reader with not one explanation of the origin of evil, as in the beginning of *Paradise Lost*, but the possibility of several factors working together, the imperfect, though perhaps not mindless, evolutionary scheme of things and man's sin of the abuse of his moral and intellectual consciousness.

Hardy's characterization of the Spirit of the Years continually undercuts the scepticism of Victorian scientific naturalism and exposes the limitations and contradictions of the agnostic, neutral stance towards reality. The aloof Spirit strikes a pose of objectivity, but as the human spectacle proceeds, the Phantom of the Years both feels and makes ethical judgments. 'Even Its official Spirit can show ruth', says the Spirit Sinister, 'At man's fag end, when his destruction's sure!' (First, VI, viii, p. 137). Clearly, the Spirit of the Years recognizes the difference between good and ill in the human world, and it often takes on the moral stance, the preaching quality, of a Huxley or Leslie Stephen. The eldest Spirit rebukes the 'lewdness' (Second, V, vii, p. 281) of Irony and dismisses the English aristocracy as a 'glib throng' (Second, II, iii, p. 195). There is a touch of comedy in Hardy's presentation of the 'official' position of the Victorian scientist, such as when he has the Spirit of the Years say to the Spirit of the Pities, 'Speak more naturally, and less in dream' (Second, VI, iv, p. 299) and in the weighty judgment that 'There lie long leagues between a woman's word— / "She will, indeed she will!"—and acting on't' (Second, VI, vii, p. 318).

As an agnostic, the Spirit of the Years ostensibly takes the position that there is no point in speculating 'on what no mind can mete' (Fore Scene, p. 2); yet it continually makes dogmatic and exclusive assumptions about the Absolute—that Its reality is monistic and that It has nothing to do with the human spirit and its ideals. Although the assumptions of Darwinism and Absolute Idealism were in the main poles apart, they did overlap in some significant ways which intrigued Hardy enough to influence his presentation of the Spirit of the Years. Both the objective idealists and the Darwinists assumed a continuity in reality and when the materialist argued for a unity of substance and the idealist for a unity of mind, the result was a case for metaphysics, implicit in the former and explicit in the latter. To avoid metaphysics, the scientist had to admit that he was ignorant of how mind and consciousness could be explained solely in physical terms. Huxley saw where a strict materialism led and conceded that if he were forced to choose between materialism and idealism, he would choose the latter.

Hardy traps the Spirit of the Years in a similar dilemma and almost brings it to make Huxley's admission. Above all the sceptical Voice wants to avoid idealism but the limitations it places on knowable reality imply the existence of a mysterious Absolute. In Herbert Spencer's words, 'To say that we cannot know the Absolute, is by implication, to affirm that there is an

Absolute.'[10] The growing scepticism of late nineteenth-century empiricism only affirmed the truth of what Hardy recorded under the heading '*Essence of Herbert Spencer*': 'Phenomenon ... without noumenon ... is unthinkable.'[11] To preserve a monistic interpretation of nature and to avoid reducing science to the analysis of feelings, theorists had somehow to account for the relation between consciousness or mind and the physical universe and to do this they began to speculate in ways that grew closer to Hartmann's analysis of the Unconscious. Even the rigid Darwinian, Ernst Haeckel, wondered if the atom might not have a primitive soul and W. K. Clifford postulated that 'Matter is a mental picture in which mind-stuff is the thing represented' ('a very attractive idea this, to me',[12] wrote Hardy) and that the universe is a vast brain.

Hardy's dramatization of the Spirit of the Years reflects the growing inadequacy, by the close of the nineteenth century, of the old certainties of materialistic determinism. The more the official Voice speaks, the more Hardy exposes its logic as restricted and restricting. It cannot help but read some aspect of mind into the Absolute and by Part III it briefly takes the idealist's position: 'What are Space and Time? A fancy!' (Third, I, iv, p. 339). In the After Scene, the eldest Spirit admits that the Semichorus of the Pities 'almost charm my long philosophy / Out of my strong-built thought, and bear me back / To when I thanks gave thus'. It once 'Knew what dreaming was, / And could let raptures rule!' (After Scene, p. 524) and though disillusioned, it still feels a kinship with the youthful Spectators' idealism and their religious conviction that more than an 'unpassioned essence' (First, I, iii, p. 17) is necessary to understand the Absolute.

All the Spirits are bound together in a gradation of thought and feeling and thus in Part I the Spirit of the Pities often assumes, at least intellectually, the main cosmic perspective of the Spirit of the Years. Influenced by the reductive cosmology, the youngest Spirit thinks that human sounds are 'Like those which thrill the hives at evenfall / When swarming pends' (First, I, ii, p. 14). The Chorus of the Pities joins in a General Chorus of Intelligences to proclaim the agnostic position that 'We may but muse on [the Will], never learn' (Fore Scene, p. 7). And the Voice of Compassion goes so far as to return the eldest Spirit's logic in kind: when the Intelligence of the Years says, 'Sprite of

Compassions, ask the Immanent!', the Spirit of the Pities replies, 'How ask the aim of unrelaxing Will / Tranced in Its purpose to unknowingness?' (First, I, ii, p. 15).

The cosmic perspective of the Voice of Pity is not simply based on intuition and feeling but also takes into account some of the 'empirical' facts and openly faces the dreary realism of the Spirit of the Years. The main difference between the two Intelligences is that over and over the cosmic emotion of the youngest pushes the intellect past the consistent boundaries generally recognized by Victorian scientists to ask the question, 'Why doth It so and so, and ever so, / This viewless, voiceless Turner of the Wheel?' (Fore Scene, p. 2). The descriptive circular answer that the Will unconsciously follows Its mechanistic laws is not enough. Is It 'Still thus? / Still thus?' (Fore Scene, p. 1); 'Why prompts the Will so senseless-shaped a doing?' (Third, VII, viii, p. 517). It is an inescapable part of being human to ask 'the perplexing fundamental questions'[13] that were by-passed in the agnostic's outlook. The problem of how to find a consistent answer is difficult, but as the overall movement of thought in the Overworld comes to question the very premises of science, Hardy opens the way to the possibility that the paths of idealism and realism might not be diverging ones after all. The very agnosticism of the Spirit of the Years leaves room for a religious conception of the Absolute, and so the Voice of Pity has the last word in Part II, expressing the hope that looks ahead to the poem's conclusion:

> Yet It may wake and understand
> Ere earth unshape, know all things, and
> With knowledge use a painless hand,
>   A painless hand.
>   (Second, VI, viii, p. 322)

From the way that Hardy has the views of his two main Spirits interlock, we can see that *The Dynasts* is his most sustained effort, and one that may be said to close out a whole era, to achieve an alliance between religion and rationality through poetry. Although the poem takes a full look at the worst, it is not meant, in its total conception, to be simply one long paean to pessimism. What Hardy had to do was to give the Spirit of the Pities' affirmation some kind of factual and rational basis, and there is a suggestion through the dramatic interchange between the Spirits that this has been achieved in the After Scene. In its hymn to a transformed Immanent Will, a Semichorus of Pities asserts,

> We hold that Thy unscanted scope
> Affords a food for final Hope,
> That mild-eyed Prescience ponders nigh
> Life's loom, to lull it by-and-by.
>
> (After Scene, p. 523)

Significantly, the Spirit of the Years comments,

> Something of difference animates your quiring,
> O half-convinced Compassionates and fond,
> From chords *consistent with our spectacle*!
>
> (After Scene, p. 524, italics mine)

If the Absolute is both Will and Idea, the Chorus of the Pities can sing of a harmonious, almost Wordsworthian, kind of nature that is the macrocosm of man's own potential being:

> The systemed suns the skies enscroll
> Obey Thee in their rhythmic roll.
> Ride radiantly at Thy command,
> Are darkened by Thy Masterhand!
>
> (After Scene, p. 523)

The poem ends appropriately with another General Chorus of all the Spirits, except the Sinister Spectre, only this time the combined Voices hymn a paean to the teleology of the human and Immanent Will. As a group the Spirits conform to Schlegel's idea of the Chorus in his *Lectures on Dramatic Art*, which Hardy read and quoted from: 'We must consider it a persistent reflection on the action which is going on; the incorporation into the representation itself of the sentiments of the poet.'[14] The final *Te Deum* combines both the idealism of the poet and the real thought of his day to express an 'Ideal-realism' rather than a consistent philosophy.

Hardy saw his use of absolutism in *The Dynasts* as a necessary step towards vindicating the reality of values, aims, and goals in the universe and he found such a reality not totally unwarranted by the facts of how evolution takes place. By ending the poem on a climactic note of teleological optimism, he did not mean to impose a solution on the philosophical and spiritual problems he had raised. His intention in *The Dynasts* was to begin to open up reality outside the prison of mechanistic determinism and the result is an emphasis on the need for a philosophy of perspectives which can do justice to the many, as yet not fully understood, aspects of the reality of nature and human nature. Just how the different cosmic perspectives mesh perfectly together and how far the range and relevance of each extends is beyond the scope of Hardy's art and is, he would say, the job of the cold ivory tower of philosophy proper with its synthesizing tools of consistent logic and argument. At least he maintains the ideal, largely through suggestion and implication, that determinism and mechanism may fall into line with a 'modicum of free will' (*PW*, p. 53) if man's cosmic outlook is broad enough to include teleology in the evolutionary process.

Undeniably the total effect of the poem is to give considerable emotional weight to the grim implications of the scientific world view and to the pattern of futility and endless bloodshed in man's history. No final, exultant hymn to creative evolution can totally erase the impression of the Will's cosmic indifference to the terrible facts of human history, but in the face of what appears to be an unalterable struggle for survival and the total bankruptcy of the Victorian belief in man's social and moral progress, Hardy maintains some hard-won truths and ideals that simply cannot be ignored in any comprehensive account of the poem. Through a subtle and careful presentation of the similarities and differences among the Voices of the Overworld, he makes two crucial points: first, that the teleological view of the Will may just have some foundation in the 'objective' facts which the Spirit of the Years believes it describes, and second, that the instrument of human consciousness which measures the facts of human nature cannot be discounted in any world view that is to guide human actions. Hardy saw that one way to show that there might be more in nature than mechanism was to dramatize the idea, the truth, that man's subjective response to the universe is never absent in any explanation of it. The Spirit of the Years' depiction of nature is a human and fallible guideline, conditioned, as with the views of the Spirits Ironic and Sinister, by a frustrated idealism. The official Spirit's professed cosmic attitude is the result of the way it looks at nature and of the cognitive map of the Immanent Brain that it draws and visualizes to enlighten the other spirits, but which can throw only a certain amount of light on nature, perhaps in one area to the exclusion of another.

The clash of the different cosmic ideas and emotions in *The Dynasts* certainly produces irony, in the sense of unresolved conflicts, but the irony points in several directions at once and which perspective finally undercuts the other is impossible to say. The total truth of the poem can emerge only from a recognition of several, as yet unresolved, truths. Given such a dilemma, however, the greatness of *The Dynasts* is that it unquestionably asserts the belief that if evolution is to have any meaning and goal, modern man must ultimately be beyond irony and a paralysis of the will. He cannot survive without spiritual ideals and a sense of ethical purpose, for without them, as in the battle of Ligny, the Apocalyptic Beast will surely descend, and not in the shape of God's wrath or Satan, but of human devolution.

NOTES

1. Thomas Hardy, 'The Dynasts: A Postscript' (1904), in *Thomas Hardy's Personal Writings*, ed. Harold Orel (1966), p. 145. Hereafter cited in the text as *PW*.

2. Thomas Hardy, *The Dynasts: An Epic-Drama of the War with Napoleon* (1965), First, VI, vii, p. 137. All further references are to this edition and will be kept parenthetically in the text with part, act, scene, and page number cited as above.

3. Frank Turner, *Between Science and Religion: The Reaction to Scientific Naturalism in Late Victorian England* (New Haven, 1974), p. 4.

4. Thomas Huxley, 'Prolegomena' (1894) to 'Evolution and Ethics' (1893), in *Selections from the Essays of T. H. Huxley*, ed. Alburey Castell (New York, 1948), p. 118.

5. Charles Darwin, *Origin of Species*, ed. J. W. Burrow (1859; Harmondsworth, 1968), p. 133.

6. Huxley, 'A Liberal Education' (1868), *Selections from the Essays of T. H. Huxley*, pp. 15–16; Tyndall, *Fragments of Science*, 6th ed. (New York, 1892), I, 132.

7. As quoted in Walter F. Wright, *The Shaping of The Dynasts* (Lincoln, 1967), pp. 48–9.

8. Eduard von Hartmann, *The Philosophy of the Unconscious: Speculative Results According to the Inductive Method of Physical Science*, trans. C. K. Ogden, 9th ed. (1931; Westport, Conn., 1972), I, xxiv. Hardy read this same translation almost certainly by 1897. Hereafter referred to in the text as *PU*.

9. In William Archer, 'Real Conversations: Conversation I—with Mr. Thomas Hardy', *Critic*, 38 (April, 1901), 316.

10. Herbert Spencer, *First Principles* (1864; New York, 1900), p. 24. Hardy quoted from *First Principles* in his ' "1867" Notebook'.

11. Entry 1335 in *The Literary Notes of Thomas Hardy: Text*, ed. Lennart A. Björk, I (Göteborg, 1974), 166.

12. W. K. Clifford, 'Body and Mind' (1874), in his *Lectures and Essays*, ed. Leslie Stephen and Frederick Pollock, 2nd ed. (1879; repr. 1886), p. 286; Hardy, Letter to Roden Noel, 3 April 1892, as quoted in Björk, *Literary Notes*, I, 365.

13. Alfred North Whitehead, *Adventures of Ideas* (New York, 1933), p. 130.

14. As quoted in William Rutland, *Thomas Hardy: A Study of His Writings and Their Background* (Oxford, 1938), p. 330.

8

Hardy and 'The Cell of Time'

by PATRICIA INGHAM

In chapter twenty-two of *A Pair of Blue Eyes*, Henry Knight finds himself by a ludicrous accident clinging for life to the edge of a cliff. Hardy then describes how—'By one of those familiar conjunctions of things wherewith the inanimate world baits the mind of man when he pauses in moments of suspense'—he sees opposite his eyes in the cliff face an imbedded fossil:

> It was a creature with eyes. The eyes, dead and turned to stone, were even now regarding him. It was one of the early crustaceans called Trilobites. Separated by millions of years in their lives, Knight and this underling seemed to have met in their place of death.[1]

Hardy draws out from this confrontation a contrast: he relates the fossil to other low types of animal existence but adds that

> The immense lapses of time each formation represented had known nothing of the dignity of man. They were grand times, but they were mean times too, and mean were their relics. He was to be with the small in his death.

This sense of the immensity of time which had pre-dated man was obviously one of the most striking revelations of nineteenth-century geology. Hardy spells it out by making Knight think back through all the stages of evolution and all the ungraspable centuries.

> Time closed up like a fan before him. He saw himself at one extremity of the years, face to face with the beginning and all the intermediate centuries simultaneously.[2]

This new grasp of time's almost unthinkable extent is used as a forceful counterpoint elsewhere in the novels, notably in *Tess of the d'Urbervilles*. What I wish to argue is, that for all the obsession with time in Hardy's poems, the geological time scheme is strangelý lacking. Only rarely as in 'The Clasped Skeletons' (858) is it used in the poetry. In place of the sense of geological time and an accompanying impression of movement, another is obsessively present in the poems: of limited and characteristically human time, unrelated to anything outside itself. Such a view of time creates, when certain recurring elements which accompany it are somehow fused and focused, some of Hardy's best and most moving poems. Crudely these might be described as claustrophobic. They are the antithesis of a number of the poems in the 1912–1913 sequence.

This is not an impression gleaned from the many direct references to time in the poems. These are, on the whole, heavy-handed attempts to emphasize, even by a capitalizing of the initial letter. But emphasis fails. The concept does not unfold. Many of these references are personifications and banal at that: 'Time the tyrant', 'dicing Time', 'the toils of Time', 'never-napping Time', 'marching Time', 'Time's transforming chisel', 'dull defacing Time'. And the personifications act predictably: 'Time the tyrant' merely 'ruled Amabel', the once beautiful. 'Dicing Time' casts 'a moan' and not 'a gladness', the 'toils of Time' carry off the 'lauded beauties' of the woman who speaks, 'never-napping Time' uses a chisel to deface the body of the speaker, 'marching Time' marks the passing of hours which reveals a broken tryst, and 'Time's transforming chisel' turns curve to crease.

It is not direct reference that reveals the grip of time on Hardy's imagination, but certain recurrent features in his treatment of it. Hynes long ago pinned Yeats' word 'antinomial' on Hardy's poetry:

> thesis ... marriage, youth, young love, the reunion of husband and wife ... is set against antithesis ... infidelity, age, death, separation ... to form an ironic complex, which is left unresolved.[3]

Hynes is concerned with the irony, the relation (ambiguous here) between appearance and reality. But when one considers the sequence in which the contrasting elements are shown, a striking aspect of Hardy's treatment of time (as opposed to his references to it) is revealed: its retrospective nature. The passing of time is seen when it has already taken place.

This is the reverse of, say, Shakespeare's sonnets on time,

where youth and beauty are present but will fade. In Hardy, conversely, the withering has already happened:

> Shadows of the October pine
> Reach into this room of mine:
> On the pine there swings a bird;
> He is shadowed with the tree.
> Mutely perched he bills no word;
> Blank as I am even is he.
> For those happy suns are past,
> Fore-discerned in winter last.
> When went by their pleasure, then?
> I, alas, perceived not when.   (273)

Priority is here given to the defacement and diminution, increased by the repetition of the chinese-box reference to another spring-winter cycle.

In this retrospective treatment, the unblemished state of things is less immediate to the imagination than the blemished. He sees 'The Faded Face' (377) and regrets that he did not 'know you young'; he presents to us the 'naked sheaf of wires' that was once 'The Sunshade' (434) and only behind it the picture of it 'silked in its white or pink' and the 'Little thumb standing against its stem'.

The justification for describing the pattern of retrospection as obsessive lies in its occurrence in poems ranging from the unsuccessful to the profound. In poems of situation, typical of *Satires of Circumstance*, events have already passed from better to worse at the moment when the speaker describes them. 'The Newcomer's Wife' (304) is already married when he discovers that his wife is 'the Hack of the Parade' and drowns himself. The girl pregnant by a married man is already married to a man she does not love when she learns on her honeymoon of the death of the lover's wife (305). The wife has already accepted her husband's ingenious present of a workbox for all her 'sewing years' before she realizes that it is made from the coffin of her lover (330).

And it is, characteristically, in retrospect and from an icy, colourless, present that the complexities of 'In Tenebris I' (136) spring:

> Wintertime nighs;
> But my bereavement-pain
> It cannot bring again:
> Twice no one dies.

Flower-petals flee;
But, since it once hath been,
No more that severing scene
Can harrow me.

Birds faint in dread:
I shall not lose old strength
In the lone frost's black length:
Strength long since fled!

Leaves freeze to dun;
But friends can not turn cold
This season as of old
For him with none.

Tempests may scath;
But love can not make smart
Again this year his heart
Who no heart hath.

Black is night's cope;
But death will not appal
One who, past doubtings all,
Waits in unhope.

Even when Hardy's viewpoint is not retrospective but forward into the future, he is inclined to a characteristic perspective. He will look forward in order to look back: to '1967' when there will be

... nothing left of me and you
In that live century's vivid view
Beyond a pinch of dust or two;   (167)

to 2000 A.D. when Max Gate will have become 'The Strange House' (537) and himself a ghost to the new inhabitants; or even 'The Minute before Meeting' (191) he looks forward to a point beyond the expected meeting when the present anticipation will be turned into looking back despondently. The future is merely a way of turning the present into the past. The ultimate in retrospective treatment comes in 'The Clock of the Years' (481), when in a sensational and ballad-like story, 'The Spirit' moves time backward to bring the lost woman back to life but ironically does not stop there: finally she is unborn.

Here in the clock poem, another recurrent feature of Hardy's view of time is associated with his retrospective view of it. Time, as elsewhere, is seen not as a corrupter but as an almost chemically negating force. It does not so much destroy as denature things, removing the natural qualities of life, warmth, colour. In 'The Dead Man Walking' (166) he describes himself:

> I am but a shape that stands here,
>   A pulseless mould,
> A pale past picture, screening
>   Ashes gone cold.   (166)

Shape has gone, pulsing life has gone, colour has gone, warmth has gone. The picture is one of that privation which reaches its ultimate in 'In Tenebris I'. And it is pictorially typical too in its reduction of everything to monochrome in a world of neutral tones, that other obsession of Hardy's.[4]

This negating, undoing force of time can produce, in his best treatment, a superb lament which is not evoked by the remains of anything once living, beautiful, young or happy:

>   Regret—though nothing dear
> That I wot of, was toward in the wide world at his prime,
>   Or bloomed elsewhere than here,
> To die with his decease, and leave a memory sweet, sublime,
>   Or mark him out in Time ....   (78)

Not even the skeleton of a sunshade starts this regret, and yet it has a power reminiscent of Shelley's *Ode to the West Wind* as, 'turning ghost', 'A Commonplace Day'

> ... scuttles from the kalendar in fits and furtively,
>   To join the anonymous host
> Of those that throng oblivion ...

The day had a 'pale, corpse-like birth', his 'colourless thoughts' of it slide like rain. Here we have a sense of pure loss because the poem has no central focus. There is no reason that Hardy can find for the feeling of privation except the negative one that (perhaps) a potential something has been crushed:

> ... maybe, in some soul,
> In some spot undiscerned on sea or land, some impulse rose,
>   Or some intent upstole

Of that enkindling ardency from whose maturer glows
     The world's amendment flows;

  But which, benumbed at birth
By momentary chance or wile, has missed its hope to be
     Embodied on the earth;
And undervoicings of this loss to man's futurity
     May wake regret in me.

There is ambivalence here: the posulated might-have-been seems
less the centre of Hardy's concern than

. . . this diurnal unit, bearing blanks in all its rays—
     Dullest of dull-hued Days!

Similarly he writes more effectively when he (typically) considers
'The Unborn' better off *not* born (235), or movingly urges the
unborn pauper child (91):

Breathe not, hid Heart: cease silently,
And though thy birth-hour beckons thee,
     Sleep the long sleep . . .

It seems a natural result of this idea of a benumbing, icing,
denaturing force that while geological time essentially moves in
order to create, this human time has little sense of movement.
Such movement as Hardy gives it is often as repetitive and
pointless as that of 'On One Who Lived and Died Where He
Was Born' (621):

Wise child of November!
     From birth to blanched hairs
Descending, ascending,
     Wealth-wantless, those stairs;
     Who saw quick in time
     As a vain pantomime
Life's tending, its ending,
     The worth of its fame.
Wise child of November,
Descending, ascending
     Those stairs!

The internal rhymes, the rapidity of the brief lines with their
almost dizzying effect, mime the futility of that ascending and
descending, however the weak expostulation ambivalently asserts
its wisdom. Something physically giddying can hardly affect us
as wise.

So Hardy's retrospective, negating, almost unmoving time leaves him usually on the wrong side of a limited stretch of existence. He is in a position not of looking forward to transience in the sense of time moving on, but almost of its opposite: stasis. Time has done its denaturing, and he is its prisoner, trapped already in the irretrievable. Once, in 'The Caged Goldfinch' (436), he merely embodies in a commonplace metaphor this strong sense of being a prisoner:

> Within a churchyard, on a recent grave,
>   I saw a little cage
> That jailed a goldfinch. All was silence save
>   Its hops from stage to stage.
>
> There was inquiry in its wistful eye,
>   And once it tried to sing;
> Of him or her who placed it there, and why,
>   No one knew anything.

Significantly the stress on the cage was here increased by Hardy when he cut out from this poem the third stanza (found in the manuscript):

> But a woman was found drowned the day ensuing,
>   And some at times averred
> The grave to be her false one's, who when wooing
>   Gave her the bird.[5]

More usual, however, than the unexplicated metaphor of the final version of 'The Caged Goldfinch' are the recurrent poems which deal specifically with being trapped in a small place. A characteristic example is 'Not Only I' (751). Here death has already come and so of course the retrospective, static, trapped state is supposed to be literally accurate:

> Not only I
> Am doomed awhile to lie
> In this close bin with earthen sides ....

As in the poems on time's transience, mentioned earlier, we here again see the joys of life at one remove, like the sunshade and its owner:

> But the things I thought, and the songs I sang,
> And the hopes I had, and the passioned pang
>   For people I knew
>   Who passed before me,

> Whose memory barely abides;
>   And the visions I drew
>   That daily upbore me!

Then a central stanza recalls these 'joyous springs and summers' and 'far-off views' only to be shut in by the third and final stanza closing trap-like, round them:

> Compressed here in six feet by two,
>   In secrecy
>   To lie with me
>   Till the Call shall be,
> Are all these things I knew . . . .

This sense of physical imprisonment is, like the retrospective view of time, one that recurs in poems of all types. It may be found in the would-be philosophical 'Fragment' (464):

> At last I entered a long dark gallery,
>   Catacomb-lined; and ranged at the side
>   Were the bodies of men from far and wide
> Who, motion past, were nevertheless not dead.

> 'The sense of waiting here strikes strong;
> Everyone's waiting, waiting, it seems to me;
>   What are you waiting for so long?—
>   What is to happen?' I said.

Or it may occur in the unspectacular picture of 'Molly Gone' (444) where the speaker sees himself, though out of doors, in a 'prison close-barred'. Or, in what sounds like an occasional piece, written 'In a Former Resort after Many Years' (666) he asks:

> Do they know me, whose former mind
> Was like an open plain where no foot falls,
> But now is as a gallery portrait-lined,
>   And scored with necrologic scrawls,
> Where feeble voices rise, once full-defined,
>   From underground in curious calls?

Time's denaturing has here already affected mind, and voices, and turned plain into prison. Or in the ballad-like story, 'Jubilate' (461), where the dead rise and dance to invisible instruments, they sing with joy—'We are out of it all!—yea, in Little-Ease cramped no more!' And in the narrative piece on 'The Clock-Winder' (471) we find the trap in fuller and characteristic form:

> It is dark as a cave,
> Or a vault in the nave
> When the iron door
> Is closed, and the floor
> Of the church relaid
> With trowel and spade.

In this setting the parish clerk ascends to wind 'the rheumatic clock' and his movement is reminiscent of the pointless 'Descending, ascending' of the stairs in 'On One Who Lived and Died Where He Was Born' (621):

> Up, up from the ground
> Around and around
> In the turret stair
> He clambers, to where
> The wheelwork is,
> With its tick, click, whizz,
> Reposefully measuring
> Each day to its end
> That mortal men spend
> In sorrowing and pleasuring.
> Nightly thus does he climb
> To the trackway of Time.

The short lines, the internal and end rhymes with their metronome-like regularity, give the lie to 'reposefully', and the thoughts of the clock-winder yearning for a dead woman are far from peaceful resignation. In fact, the earliest version of the poem had no reference to a lost lover.[6]

The trap is here found in a form that I have suggested is more characteristic of Hardy because it is an interior. His *Huis Clos* is, essentially, the house, the room. His finest claustrophobic poems, in which the obsessive sense of being trapped by unmoving time is embodied in an interior, make us grasp almost painfully what he meant in *A Pair of Blue Eyes* by 'those familiar conjunctions of things wherewith the inanimate world baits the

mind of man'. Shut in, he confronts 'Old Furniture' (428) which
surrounds him:

> I know not how it may be with others
>   Who sit amid relics of householdry
> That date from the days of their mothers' mothers,
>   But well I know how it is with me
>   Continually.
>
> I see the hands of the generations
>   That owned each shiny familiar thing
> In play on its knobs and indentations,
>   And with its ancient fashioning
>   Still dallying . . .

The furniture serves to mock the human beings whose memory
it recalls as

> Hands behind hands, growing paler and paler,
>   As in a mirror a candle-flame
> Shows images of itself, each frailer
>   As it recedes, though the eye may frame
>   Its shape the same.

The undoing effect of time is captured along with the sense of
being trapped within this permanently furnished room.

Similarly there is all the domestic intensity of Emily Dickinson
in his picture of the man shut up in the house with a figure left
colourless and formless by time.

> We two kept house, the Past and I,
>   The Past and I;
> Through all my tasks it hovered nigh,
>   Leaving me never alone.
> It was a spectral housekeeping
>   Where fell no jarring tone,
> As strange, as still a housekeeping
>   As ever has been known.   (249)

There is the familiar ambivalence of the statement that there
was 'no jarring tone' contrasting with the pointlessly repetitive
movement which follows:

> As daily I went up the stair
>   And down the stair . . . .

As elsewhere, the past is dimly seen through the ravages of the present now that

> gaunt griefs had torn old troths
> And dulled old rapturings.

The personified figure of the Past itself, of course, 'dwindles' into a 'far-off skeleton'.

But the poem which, above all, expresses through a stifling domestic interior the claustrophobic trap into which time has shut the speaker and from which all except pointless, giddying movement is excluded is 'The Masked Face' (473):

> I found me in a great surging space,
>   At either end a door,
> And I said: 'What is this giddying place,
>   With no firm-fixéd floor,
>   That I knew not of before?'
> 'It is Life,' said a mask-clad face.
>
> I asked: 'But how do I come here,
>   Who never wished to come;
> Can the light and air be made more clear,
>   The floor more quietsome,
>   And the doors set wide? They numb
> Fast-locked, and fill with fear.'

This question is mockingly answered in the third and final stanza by an opaque statement:

> The mask put on a bleak smile then,
>   And said, 'O vassal-wight,
> There once complained a goosequill pen
>   To the scribe of the Infinite
>   Of the words it had to write
> Because they were past its ken.'

This trite assertion, that he cannot understand because he is an uncomprehending instrument, seems to shut him in more securely.

The isolation that a prisoner feels is suggested ironically by the very presence of the masked face. And so too it is in 'Who's

in the Next Room?' (450), said by Purdy[7] to have been identified
as taking place at Max Gate:

> 'Who's in the next room?—who?
>   I seemed to see
> Somebody in the dawning passing through,
>   Unknown to me.

That this is not another prisoner attempting to communicate is
made clear by the following chilling stanzas:

> 'Who's in the next room?—who?
>   I seem to hear
> Somebody muttering firm in a language new
>   That chills the ear.'
> 'No: you catch not his tongue who has entered there.'

> 'Who's in the next room?—who?
>   I seem to feel
> His breath like a clammy draught, as if it drew
>   From the Polar Wheel.'
> 'No: none who breathes at all does the door conceal.'

It is also made clear that the next room contains the figure of
death and horrors worse than this one:

> 'Who's in the next room?—who?
>   A figure wan
> With a message to one in there of something due?
>   Shall I know him anon?'
> 'Yea he; and he brought such; and you'll know him anon.'

The ballad form reminiscent in its development of 'Edward' (or
'Lord Randal'), captures the sinister note superbly. The door to
the next room hardly tempts the prisoner to open it.

The dramatizing of an attempt to break out of the stifling,
enclosed space is found in 'A Wasted Illness' (122) where physical
distemper and the building become fused:

> Through vaults of pain,
> Enribbed and wrought with groins of ghastliness,
> I passed, and garish spectres moved my brain
>   To dire distress.

> And hammerings,
> And quakes, and shoots, and stifling hotness, blent
> With webby waxing things and waning things
>   As on I went.

He sees an apparent end to 'this foul way' in a door ahead, 'The door to Death', but it slips from him—

> And back slid I
> Along the galleries by which I came,
> And tediously the day returned, and sky,
> And life—the same.

Yet he still knows that the same movement must be made—

> And those grim chambers, must be ranged again
> To reach that door.

In contrast to 'Who's in the Next Room?' there is the muffled suggestion here that death might be a way out. But the relief appears uncertain and ambiguous.

Only in the poem on his mother's death is he able to convey a sense that death is a relief, a breaking out from the trap into which his static view of time seems to lock humanity: again gazing round a domestic interior he sees the persisently surviving inanimate things; the creased sheets, pillows, and

> The lettered vessels of medicaments
> Seem asking wherefore we have set them here;   (223)

but this time they are conquered by the pervading sense of relief:

> Each palliative its silly face presents
> As useless gear.

> And yet we feel that something savours well;
> We note a numb relief withheld before;
> Our well-beloved is prisoner in the cell
> Of Time no more.

The mere escape is enough, 'the deft achievement', and the poem dwells on the sense of ease at the fact that

> There's no more to be done, or feared, or hoped . . . .

It does not focus on what lies beyond 'the cell of Time'.

Only here does the escape asserted seem to be conveyed as real. This is not so in those poems which try to assert that there is an escape from time possible by other means. They make use of the idea used, for instance, in Shakespeare's sonnets that one lives on through descendants and so transcends time's limits. This idea is plainly stated in 'Heredity' (363):

> I am the family face;
> Flesh perishes, I live on,
> Projecting trait and trace
> Through time to times anon,
> And leaping from place to place
> Over oblivion.
>
> The years-heired feature that can
> In curve and voice and eye
> Despise the human span
> Of durance—that is I;
> The eternal thing in man,
> That heeds no call to die.

But this, despite its assertiveness, is oddly self-contradictory, since the life that heredity perpetuates is still seen as 'the human span / Of durance'.

More convincing is the negative implication of the idea drawn out in 'Sine Prole' (690), that because he is without offspring the potential transcending of time will fail:

> Forth from ages thick in mystery,
> Through the morn and noon of history,
>   To the moment where I stand
> Has my line wound: I the last one—
> Outcome of each spectral past one
>   Of that file, so many-manned!

But no poem accepting that by heredity of flesh or spirit man transcends his 'span of durance' carries the force of those poems in which such an idea visibly crumbles as the speaker attempts to expand it.

In 'His Immortality' (109) this is precisely what happens:

I

> I saw a dead man's finer part
> Shining within each faithful heart
> Of those bereft. Then said I: 'This must be
>   His immortality.'

II

> I looked there as the seasons wore,
> And still his soul continuously bore
> A life in theirs. But less its shine excelled
> Than when I first beheld.

III

> His fellow-yearsmen passed, and then
> In later hearts I looked for him again;
> And found him—shrunk, alas! into a thin
> And spectral mannikin.

IV

> Lastly I ask—now old and chill—
> If aught of him remain unperished still;
> And find, in me alone, a feeble spark,
> Dying amid the dark.

The characteristic denaturing and 'dwindling' of the man represents a crumbling before our eyes of the thesis that he can live on through his descendants, and so transcend the cell of time. Such a development carries all the conviction that the poems asserting transcendence through heredity lack.

The negative idea is as compelling here as in the situation poem 'The Pedigree' (390). There the written pedigree itself mocks the speaker physically:

> The branches seemed to twist into a seared and cynic face
> Which winked and tokened towards the window like a Mage
> Enchanting me to gaze again thereat.

What he sees in the window is the powerful image of the mirror showing, as usual, man dwindling:

III

> It was a mirror now,
> And in it a long perspective I could trace
> Of my begetters, dwindling backward each past each
> All with the kindred look,
> Whose names had since been inked down in their place
> On the recorder's book,
> Generation and generation of my mien, and build, and brow.

The mirror then suddenly seems to become one more inanimate object which 'baits the mind of man':

IV

> And then did I divine
> That every heave and coil and move I made
> Within my brain, and in my mood and speech,
>   Was in the glass portrayed
> As long forestalled by their so making it . . . .

There is a sense here of action being so predetermined that it enwraps him like a snake, in whose grip he heaves and coils like a snake himself. He is trapped, not released, by the written pedigree: time's stasis is inescapable. So, at least, the poem convinces us as it reasserts the familiar claustrophobia. The only movement, as before, is a backward, dwindling one.

And in this poem, as in several others, the metre and diction underline the effect of the trap. In some, as has been pointed out, the jingling metre enacts the repetitive, pointless movement. In others including 'The Pedigree', 'The Masked Face' and 'A Wasted Illness' there is a characteristic effect of impeded movement. This is created either by qualifications and inversions like

> Through vaults of pain,
> Enribbed and wrought with groins of ghastliness,
> I passed . . .

or by consonant groups which are difficult to enunciate as in a 'mask-clad face'. The metre is slow and cumbersome often in Hardy's poems, but here to a purpose.

Similarly, adding to the effect in these poems, is the scattering of archaism. When the masked face answers the speaker's question as to why he has been brought to the 'giddying place' it says obliquely:

> O vassal-wight,
> There once complained a goosequill pen
>   To the scribe of the Infinite
>   Of the words it had to write
> Because they were past its ken.

The phrases 'O vassal-wight' and 'past its ken' are archaic-poetic. An archaism is a dead word revived. It carries with it to any native speaker an element of artificiality. It is felt as a sterile form, not part of a usable language; it is essentially static by contrast with other words. Such sterility fits perfectly where man is seen in an artificial and virtually inescapable trap. And what is true of 'vassal-wight' and 'past its ken' is true also of the trivial archaic forms *ere, yea, nay, troths, whilom, blent* which sprinkle the other poems under discussion. Consider for instance:

> And hammerings,
> And quakes, and shoots, and stifling hotness, blent
> With webby waxing things and waning things . . .

where *blent* is used for the more normal *mixed*. The increase in artificiality is self-evident. It refutes the idea sometimes expressed that in Hardy archaic words 'serve to shift the tone upward and out of time'.[8] A word which cannot be used freely, which is in effect a verbal fossil, is locked in time. Only when it recalls an earlier, specific and powerful context, as does Keats' ironic use of *trammel up* in *Lamia*, can it open up associations. The very triviality of Hardy's archaisms works against this.

In summary, I have described the recurring features of Hardy's treatment of time which occur, sometimes separately, sometimes fused together, as that it is retrospective, denaturing, static, claustrophobic and largely inescapable. There is no development to be traced in these obsessive qualities: they may occur as early as the 1880s in 'A Wasted Illness', or as late as 'The Pedigree' (which was not published, at least, till 1917). The 'cell of time' seems to have been a constant in Hardy's poems including many not cited.

It accounts perhaps for the added sense of release found in some of Hardy's best poems in the 1912–1913 sequence, written after Emma's death and recalling the past in a way which in almost every respect differs from that outlined above; it is more vivid than the present and more alive, full of a sense of movement and freedom and usually in an outdoor setting. There is, indeed, one poem (740), which clearly belongs with the 1912–13 group[9] and which marks the transition:

> She opened the door of the West to me,
> With its loud sea-lashings,
> And cliff-side clashings
> Of waters rife with revelry.

> She opened the door of Romance to me,
>   The door from a cell
>   I had known too well,
> Too long, till then, and was fain to flee.
>
> She opened the door of a Love to me,
>   That passed the wry
>   World-welters by
> As far as the arching blue the lea.
>
> She opens the door of the Past to me,
>   Its magic lights,
>   Its heavenly heights,
> When forward little is to see!

For once the way out of the present was the past which here expanded instead of dwindling. So, the 1912–13 poems seem to constitute stepping out of the cell.

NOTES

1. Wessex Edition, p. 241.
2. *Ibid.*, p. 242.
3. S. Hynes, *The Pattern of Hardy's Poetry* (Chapel Hill, 1961), p. 44.
4. See No. 79 in *The Complete Poems*: 'At a Lunar Eclipse'.
5. *Ibid.*, p. 963.
6. *Ibid.*, p. 963.
7. R. L. Purdy, *Thomas Hardy: A Bibliographical Study* (Oxford, 1968), p. 202.
8. Hynes, pp. 104–5.
9. It was published in *Human Shows* in 1925.

'Unlawful Beauty': Order and Things in Hardy's Poems

by PATRICIA CLEMENTS

Hardy's later work is dominated by its inquiry into the relation of the mind to the world it inhabits. *Jude the Obscure* carries his inquiry to its most successful expression in fiction. Jude's vision of Christminster, his purely personal mental act, is the steady surface against which the novel's events are imaged, the unchanging measure of the shifting realities of his life. Jude renews his vision again and again, in spite of evidence returned to him by his experience, and the novel derives its resonance from its steadily maintained discrepancy between Jude's dream and his life. The book takes Hardy's dominant theme to its best balance in imaginative prose: it shows the mind locked in permanent contest with the world, focusing each in relation to the other, and it does that without tempting us to see the objects of the real world as merely the objects of consciousness and without throwing into doubt the conventions of its own realism. In other work of about the same time, Hardy dismantled the equipoise, in what appears as experiment or witty play, placing his perfected powers now at the disposal of a fictional treatment of the mind wielding its triumphs over the 'real', now of a treatment of the 'real' as sufficient. Though he said that he hoped that Jocelyn Pierston would not appear to readers of *The Well-Beloved* as merely a 'fantast', he did describe him as 'one that gave objective continuity and a name to a delicate dream', and he said that the story itself was 'of an ideal or subjective nature, and frankly imaginative, verisimilitude . . . [having] been subordinated to [that] aim'.[1] In other late prose works, Hardy tipped the balance of *Jude* in the other direction, boldly clinging to the conventions of realistic fiction by the unusual means of simply converting the 'dream' to the 'real', of simply asserting the impossible as fact. The fine story, 'An Imaginative Woman', for instance (which mentions in passing the French Symbolist school), offers Hardy's symbolism *as* science, and he claims in the preface to *Life's Little Ironies* that the tale's central event (which a reader must recognize as symbolically eloquent but physically preposterous) was 'well known to medical practitioners'.[2] In the preface to *Wessex Tales*, too, Hardy treats his reader to a witty demonstration of his concern for facts, confessing what he calls an error in his memory of the story which he turned into 'The Withered Arm'. It was in the afternoon, he says, and not in the evening, that Rhoda Brook was 'oppressed' by an incubus. He offers his error in remembering as an example of the inevitable divergence of the mind from the world, as

> an instance of how our imperfect memories insensibly formalize the fresh originality of living fact—from whose shape they slowly depart, as machine-made castings depart by degrees from the sharp hand-work of the mould.[3]

The unceasing play between the mind's 'formalizations' and the world's 'originality' occupies every side of Hardy's art. His description here of that play reverses expectation: it may be a surprise to hear, from this 'novelist of the imagination',[4] this poet of vision, that it is the world, and not the mind, which is shifting, original, alive; that it is the mind, and not the world, which tends mechanically, by degrees, to stiffen experience with pattern.

When Hardy moved entirely to poetry, he did not abandon his dominant theme. The mastered antitheses of *Jude*, which he had split into singleness in some of his other late fiction, provide the counterpoint and the balance of the poems—and if the poems do aim at a multiplied counterpoint, as Hardy's prefaces frequently suggest, they also aim at balance, at a presentation of the mind *in* the world. Their concern with balance makes them consistent not only with Hardy's fiction, but also with other aspects of his thought. It is the relation of the mind to the world which fascinates his notebooks, occupies as its central aesthetic question his late essay on 'The Science of Fiction', constitutes the focus of his reading in psychology. At about the same time as Yeats was drawing up his powerful design for a poetry which would exclude 'mere reality',[5] Hardy was striving to write poems which would be, as he said more than once, an 'exploration of reality';[6]

and while Yeats was making room for Eliot to appear as his natural opposite by rejecting utterly a poetry of 'observations',[7] Hardy was taking care to present his 'series of feelings and fancies' together with 'diverse readings of [life's] phenomena'.[8] His poems, Hardy said in the year in which *The Waste Land* was published, were mediations between kinds of experience, attempts to embody the unifying dream of 'an alliance between religion, which must be retained unless the world is to perish, and complete rationality, which must come, unless the world also is to perish, by the interfusing effect of poetry.'[9] In spite of his several comments about its 'lack of concord',[10] Hardy's poetry does aim at a precarious wholeness, at 'interfusion' of kinds of experience, and at observation of the complex inter-lacings of the mind and the world.

Hardy's poems create their central drama, their drama of many characters and impersonations, out of the conflict between an actively searching intelligence and the evidence which is returned to it by experience. They are fascinated by observation of the 'interaction between seeing and knowing and expecting'.[11] They include of course moments of vision, in which experience delivers directly an intense or sufficient feeling. But what the mind sees, with whatever degree of intensity, is, as a dramatic or personative poetry is calculated to show, only part of what exists to be seen, and many of Hardy's poems record the consequences of a second glance, of information uncovered after conclusions have already been drawn. They present moments in which experience expands, so that the mind must in response either open or close, re-draw its design of the world or confirm its isolation in its formalization of what it has seen before. Hardy's poems detail a process of the un-making and re-making of meaning—or of a 'frail-witted' and 'illuded' (31) refusal to do that—and they show the poet, as himself or as a character in whom he masks his quest, obliged, over and over, to abandon conclusion and start again. The characters of Hardy's poems, like One-Eyed Riley's patients, very often learn that they are 'strangers', very often discover from their confrontations with the fresh originality of living fact that they are 'nothing but a set / Of obsolete responses'.[12] In this essay, I want to examine some of the ways in which Hardy measures and corrects the mind's formalizations by submitting its experience to reconsideration.

Hardy treats the experience of the reconstruction of meaning dramatically in his almost obsessive pattern of repetition or return. Like Jude, whose heavenly vision draws him back in a painful rhythm to his earthly city, or like Jocelyn, whose fantasy drives him restlessly back to Portland, the characters in his poems come back. Sometimes they come back to voice a simple *ubi sunt* theme, to learn that 'Time's transforming chisel' (152) has been at work on the scene; sometimes they come back to find that the scene itself has been held static, but that it measures change in them. In both cases, they return to discover, and sometimes to correct, the shocking separateness of the life of the mind from the life of things, to learn how the mind has, insensibly, stylized its own experience. In these moments of re-vision, Hardy isolates the mind in an experience of shock, of thrilling perception, and he forces it to reorganize or retreat.

Hardy's poems of return make their effect by exploiting a natural 'tension' or 'conflict' between 'the perception of order and the perception of things'.[13] Repetition creates pattern, of course: the kaleidoscope, as E. H. Gombrich points out, transforms our 'messy environment' into 'a thing of lawful beauty'. But repetition also creates a precise expectation of order and it deprives individual things of their identities. When Hardy sends his questing figure back, he pits a clearly defined expectation against his character's capacity to see what is before him, and he submits that 'order' to the possibility of complete revision. In repetition, the mind's stiff patterning can be shattered as it cannot be in experience which involves no very rigid expectation. Ordinary experience in time can merely confirm or extend or amplify or qualify a hypothetical order, but repetition can submit an achieved pattern to total judgement. (It can also permit a poet to treat time as though it were space and experience as though it were design.) Since it can result in a complete destruction of pattern and order, can leave a returning figure naked of artifice, there is a sense in which repetition can offer the only really *new* experience.

Hardy pares his poems of return to the barest-possible shape. They consist of the pattern and the perceiver, and they make their shattering point simply by failing to repeat one element in the pattern. Hardy underlines the repeated elements carefully. In 'The Revisitation' (152), for instance, he details the similarities between the present night and the night of twenty years before: the pee-wits, the bridge, the lane, the 'upper roadway', the 'open drouthy downland', the 'spry white scuts of conies', the Sarsen stone—all of those things are 'the same'. They are, the speaking soldier tells us, things 'I knew so well'; they are 'familiar'; they exist 'as before'. The speaking wanderer in 'The Voices of Things' returns three times to the same spot to create in *us* the clear expectation that the waves of the sea will continue to voice his feelings. The speaker of 'My Cicely' rides twice along the same path, forth and back through a landscape whose important details are repeated. In 'Where the Picnic Was' (297), the poet climbs to the empty circle by the straight line by which he gained the hill a year before. It is, he says, 'the same'. The emphasized repetitions are important. 'The perception of regularity, of repetition and redundancy,' E. H. Gombrich writes, 'presents a great economy':

> Faced with an array of identical objects, whether they are the beads of a necklace, the paving stones of a street, or the columns of a building, we rapidly form the preliminary hypothesis that we are confronted with a lawful assembly . . . .[14]

It is for the purpose of establishing that preliminary hypothesis that Hardy's poems are so carefully repetitive. Their patterning is precise, insistent, emphasized: his characters have a right to expect that it will also be complete.

In his poems of return, Hardy makes the repeating action of the present into a kind of transparency, a tracing of the action of the past through which we look to see order confirming itself. But however persuaded Hardy's returning characters (or his readers) may be that what is before them is what should be there, they are forced finally to see something which is not a part of the lawful assembly, to recognize a moment at which the tracing and the experience do not match. The jolt is always provided by an unconforming object, by a thing which threatens to overpower the mind's perception of order. It is the naked objectivity of the thing which shocks us, and Hardy frequently heightens the shock by suddenly turning into a *thing* something we prefer to see in other than an objective light—the very notation of meaning, say, in 'Her Initials' (11), or a person, as in 'The Dream-Follower'

(108), in which 'my old Love' becomes 'but a thing of flesh and bone / Speeding on to its cleft in the clay.'

Hardy emblematized the central, repeated, frustrating experience of his poems in the drawing of the broken key which he placed over 'Nature's Questioning' (43) in *Wessex Poems*. It is illustrated with nice economy in 'Her Initials', a poem in which the object of sense is drained of significance before our very eyes:

> Upon a poet's page I wrote
> Of old two letters of her name;
> Part seemed she of the effulgent thought
> Whence that high singer's rapture came.
> —When now I turn the leaf the same
> Immortal light illumes the lay,
> But from the letters of her name
> The radiance has waned away!

This poem arrests attention by its sudden final movement, which wrenches 'the letters of her name' out of every context and turns them into mere things. But the movement is achieved by a carefully controlled motionlessness, by precisely repetitive form and language. Hardy breaks the poem into two, but he locks its two halves together by sameness. The rhyme, the strategic, emphatic location of the word, 'same', and the near-mirroring of the second line in the second-last line keep the similarities steadily before us. Furthermore, the very imagery which conveys loss of significance is the imagery which conveys stability of meaning: the 'radiance' of the letters has 'waned', but the 'lay' is still 'illumined'. What has changed is the object's relation to everything else in the poem. It is no longer part of the 'effulgent thought', no longer in the same relation to the speaker. Hardy isolates the object of sense—the letters, which are kept nakedly as objects by being only letters and not words—by a process which is the opposite of the creation of literary symbolism. In this poem, and in very many others, he de-symbolizes the object, taking it out of a pattern, lifting it away from its contexts. His purpose, here and elsewhere, is to show the mind forced to revise its contact with things and to bring its description of experience up to date.

Hardy takes the *motif* of return to its dramatic antitheses in 'My Cicely' (31) and 'The Revisitation' both of which submit their central character to a measuring repetition for the purpose of observing him in the moment at which experience overpowers expectation. In both poems, the crisis is described as a moment of disorientation: the rider in 'My Cicely' is driven into a lengthy 'self-colloquy' and the more self-conscious soldier of 'The Revisitation' is dazzled by light: 'But it *may* be (though I know not) that this trick on us of Time / Disconcerted and confused me', he says. It is also presented as a moment of moral choice: these seekers can choose to see or to dream. 'My Cicely' submits its rider to two crises: he is drawn mourning from the city (where he has 'squandered green years and maturer / In bowing the knee / To Baals illusive and specious') by news that his lover is dead. He arrives at the rural scene which is his goal, however, to learn that 'Time's repartee' has been much wittier than he had thought possible: his Cicely is not dead after all, but so unlike his memory of her (the 'Canon's kinswoman' has 'wedded beneath her' and turned into a barmaid) that he is unable to recognize her when she actually appears before his eyes. For him, the lesser change seems the greater: although his Cicely is not dead, she has changed from the 'Fair Unforgotten' to 'That Thing'. Choosing to regard her change as a 'hocus satiric'[15] of dark power, he recoils, backtracks, turns the 'Thing' back into the 'Fair Unforgotten', and returns to the city of illusion. He would rather, he says, seem 'frail-witted' than let his mind receive as true what his eye saw: 'Far better / To dream than to own the debasement / Of sweet Cicely.'

This poem is not, I think, a proposal that 'life has meaning only to the extent that one imagines it for oneself.'[16] This romantic rider's 'self-colloquy' (or reverie, dream, illusion, half-consciousness—these are forms of words which appear in the poem) commits him to death, and Hardy makes the poem's double return serve the purpose of judgement. For the rider, nothing changes: when he rides West, he rides towards 'her my mindsight / Saw stretched pallidly'; when he rides East, he rides towards 'she of the garth, who lay rapt in / Her long reverie.' Both are trips through a landscape of death (the 'cromlechs unstoried, / And lynchets, and sepultured Chieftains') which, as is usual in Hardy, reflect the speaker's internal state. But Hardy delivers a harsh verdict on his self-communing character, and his landscapes make that clear, too. When his rider is finally confirmed in illusion, Hardy produces a landscape which is not merely a reflection of his character's state of mind, but a sharp comment on his isolation:

> So, lest I disturb my choice vision,
>   I shun the West Highway,
> Even now, when the knaps ring with rhythms
>   From blackbird and bee . . . .

The blackbird and bee and the rhythm represent the intrusion into the rider tranced monologue of the poet's sharpness, and they mock his static, deathly dream. This character abandons the quest which is central to Hardy's verse, gives up his negotiations with reality, and Hardy condemns him for it.

The 'war-worn stranger' of 'The Revisitation' (152), which appeared as the first poem in *Time's Laughingstocks*, is the romantic rider's antithesis. This traveller believes what he sees, comes to a painful self-recognition, and abandons his 'romantic notion'.

> Did I not return, then, ever?—
> Did we meet again?—mend all?—Alas, what greyhead
>   perseveres!—
> Soon I got the Route elsewhither.

The different responses of the rider and the soldier are conveyed most clearly in the treatments of the changed women who provoke their crises. The real Cicely appears in a single stanza, as a remembered glance, as two or three details which are quickly succeeded by the prolonged self-colloquy of the speaker. Agnette of 'The Revisitation', however, takes shape in a series of brilliantly detailed stages which separate her by regular steps from the soldier's fantasy and make her the poem's most striking feature. She begins as an unnamed memory, as 'One who went'; she assumes the shape of the soldier's fancy, emerging merely as one of the repeating details of a pattern; and she concludes as a figure fully alive in the present, detached from fantasy, telling the truth. ' "—Yes, Sir, I am *old*," said she'. When Agnette first appears, she issues from a landscape whose dark repeating details have confirmed the 'sleepless swain of fifty' in his dream of recovering the past. She is presented as the final, fulfilling repetition and as the embodiment of his dream:

> ... my eyes discerned there, suddenly,
> That a figure broke the skyline—first in vague contour, then
> stronger,
> And was crossing near to me.
>
> Some long-missed familiar gesture,
> Something wonted, struck me in the figure's pause to list and
> heed,
> Till I fancied from its handling of its loosely wrapping vesture
> That it might be She indeed.

But when, after the fantasy-confirming night, the 'red upedging sun' returns the soldier to consciousness, it reveals the fine features of the landscape ('the meanest mound and mole-hill' and 'trails the ewes had beat'), and it sharply separates Agnette from his fantasy, revealing her specifically as an object: 'Can you really wince and wonder / That the sunlight should reveal you such a thing of skin and bone,' she asks him. Her reality, her objectivity, makes him abandon the broken pattern of his fantasy. The verbs describe a moment of self-recognition:

> Well I knew my native weakness,
> Well I know it still. I cherished her reproach like physic-wine,
> For I saw in that emaciate shape of bitterness and bleakness
> A nobler soul than mine.

This questor's bitter enlightenment distinguishes him utterly from the romantic rider of 'My Cicely'. While he condemns the one figure to ride a repeated, pallid road, Hardy sets the other free: 'Soon I got the Route elsewhither.'

Moments in which Hardy's characters are 'arrested by perceptions such as these' (940) are often carried in an imagery of fire or strong light. The light of 'Her Initials', which wanes as the object is drained of significance, is the negative example, suggesting the speaker's loss of contact with the object of contemplation, but the remembered vitality and engagement of 'The Self-Unseeing' (135) circles an imagery of fire—

> She sat here in her chair,
> Smiling into the fire;
> He who played stood there,
> Bowing it higher and higher

—and the emotion of 'The Oxen' (403) takes its warmth from the 'embers' of the first stanza. The flashing light of the world reveals the pallor of fantasy. 'Self-Unconsciousness' (270), for instance, in which the speaker passes through the world oblivious to everything but 'shapes that reveries limn', makes his abstraction flimsy and pale beside the 'mirthful clamours' of the world. His 'half-wrapt eye' sees only 'projects' and 'specious plans', and fails to perceive the 'bright yellowhammers' and the 'smooth sea-line / With a metal shine, / And flashes of white' of 'the moment that encompassed him'. The world, when it is seen, is intense with moving light, but often the light is edged with flame. The face of the real Cicely, which shatters the pale dream of the poem's rider, is 'liquor-fired'; the sun which reveals the creases in Agnette's face is 'red, upedging'; the moment which blinds the bird is a 'stab of fire' (375). The light of fantasy, it appears, is pale and watery, but moments at which the mind grasps the world outside itself are moments of fire, often painful.

'Where the Picnic Was' (297) is one of Hardy's richest poems of return. It embodies the repeated quest of the *Collected Poems*, shows the poet actively searching the landscape for sense:

> I slowly climb
> Through winter mire,
> And scan and trace
> The forsaken place
> Quite readily.

The elements of the poem's pattern are explicitly geometrical and perfectly balanced. Its opening and closing stanzas organize their recovered details around a repeated 'strange straight line / Up hither' to point directly at the central, second stanza which presents as its central image the empty circle:

> Now a cold wind blows,
> And the grass is gray,
> But the spot still shows
> As a burnt circle—aye,
> And stick-ends, charred,
> Still strew the sward
> Whereon I stand,
> Last relic of the band
> Who came that day!

Like the two 'letters of her name', the 'burnt circle' is an emblem for the shifting relation of the mind to the world, for the constant crumbling and remaking of meaning. It takes its sense from its complex relation to the other two stanzas. We know from the first that it was a circle of fire; we know from the last that it suggests the lost circle of four, the broken 'band' (that is also a circle when it is a wedding band) of people who made the picnic the year before. The 'burnt circle' and 'stick-ends, charred' are, like the poet, 'relics' of those other circles; the circle and the charred sticks, and so, we conclude, the poet, are drained of substance, consumed. Only the remembered fire is vivid with colour in this poem. The stick-ends are black; the 'grass is gray'. This poem lays the perfectly transparent pattern of the present over the pattern of the past. Its burnt circle is perfectly precise, perfectly suggestive: it has 'the suggestiveness of true poetry'—an 'aura around a bright clear centre.'[17]

Hardy's fascination with the constant re-shaping of sense appears in his attraction to a kind of progressive redefinition of the words he uses. The word, *wild* which appears three times in 'Domicilium' (1), his 'earliest known production in verse', is an example. It is the shifting degree of 'wildness' which creates this poem's irony and gives force to its ideas of change and permanence. The word occurs first as a romanticized detail in the poet's own description of his ancestral home: 'Wild honeysucks / Climb on the walls,' he says, 'and seem to sprout a wish . . . / To overtop the apple-trees hard by'. It reappears in his description of the surrounding landscape: 'Behind,' he says, 'the scene is wilder. Heath and furze / Are everything that seem to grow and thrive / Upon the uneven ground.' And it occurs for the last time after Hardy has performed a double leap backwards in time, to remember in his past his grandmother describing her past. In the fifty years since she 'first settled here', she explains, 'change has marked / The face of all things':

> Our house stood quite alone, and those tall firs
> And beeches were not planted. Snakes and efts
> Swarmed in the summer days, and nightly bats
> Would fly about our bedrooms. Heathcroppers
> Lived on the hills, and were our only friends;
> So wild it was when first we settled here.

The effect is dramatic irony: the 'wild honeysucks' of the first stanza, which seemed quite wild enough in their place, have been made now to seem very domestic indeed. The poem has deprived the word of its first force, and so the reader of *The Collected Poems* encounters at the outset what will reappear throughout, a sense of the 'originality' of the world outstripping any attempt to formalize it in description. 'Long Plighted' (105) plays for similar effect on the first word of its title, expanding and contracting the possible length of 'long', lifting it finally from the modest context of betrothal to the expanded context of the life of the world, when one of the waiting partners asks

> Is it worth while, dear, since
> As mates in Mellstock churchyard we can lie,
> Till the last crash of all things low and high
> Shall end the spheres?

And 'The Blinded Bird' (375), relocating I Corinthians xiii, empties it of one sense to fill it bitterly with another. The reconstruction of meaning is the object of the triolet, whose formal requirement is that context should be made twice to shift the sense of the opening phrase. The attraction of the form consists entirely in its rapid undoing and redoing of meaning and in its paradoxical use of repetition to convey change. 'The Birds at Winter Nightfall' (115) accumulates speed in its constant reshapings of sense:

> Around the house the flakes fly faster,
> And all the berries now are gone
> From holly and cotonea-aster
> Around the house. The flakes fly!—faster
> Shutting indoors that crumb-outcaster
> We used to see upon the lawn
> Around the house. The flakes fly faster,
> And all the berries now are gone!

Hardy's consistent re-making of the significance of experience appears movingly in the ballads and narratives of *Wessex Poems*, in which he submits world events to local reconsideration, lifting the Battle of Waterloo, or the Battle of the Khyber Pass, out of the impersonal context of text-book history to relocate it in the complex emotional territory of the lives of his Wessex characters. In these poems, Hardy makes his reconstruction theme serve his anti-heroic impulse. They are laced with a satire which takes as its object not their small, speaking characters, but a view which is sufficiently grand to think that human events are ever not personal. In 'Leipzig' (24), Hardy approaches the historical event itself by a double displacement from the heroic centre which is occupied by the 'One, care-tossed'. We are told of the battle not by 'Old Norbert', the migrated German, but by, as he quotes her, his mother, and Hardy emphasizes the complex distance and proximity of the teller and the tale. What Old Norbert remembers as chiefly affecting about his mother is what is least historically remarkable—

> . . . her voice and mien
> When she used to sing and pirouette,
> And tap the tambourine
>
> To the march that yon street-fiddler plies . . .

and it is the march, the music of the present, which prompts him to tell his version of the monumental event. 'The Peasant's Confession' (25), similarly, revises history into a personal tale, explaining what the textbooks omit, supplying in the personal view of the confessing peasant a meaning which has been denied to the limited mind of history. In the powerful 'San Sebastian' (21), Hardy makes personal history acidly anti-heroic. It is the object before the old soldier's eyes—the 'comely maid' who 'danced in her muslin bowed with blue, / Round a Hintock maypole'—which reminds him of the violent horror of his war-time heroism. The poem is constructed for subversion: the soldier remembers an accumulation of details which should assure his auditor of a satisfying tale of heroic action. 'We'd stormed it at night, by the flapping light / Of burning towers', he says. 'From the battered hornwork the cannoneers / Hove crashing balls of iron fire'. But at the top of his climb to victory the soldier finds a woman with 'beseeching eyes', and the issue of this combat is plunder and rape. The eyes of the past dominate the present. Hardy makes use here of the 'phenomenon' of 'An Imaginative Woman', giving the soldier's daughter the eyes of the woman he raped: 'For the mother of my child', he says, 'is not / The mother of her eyes.' The violent fire of war is transformed:

> I delight me not in my proud career;
> And 'tis coals of fire that a gracious wife
> Should have brought me a daughter dear!

In his 'Poems of Pilgrimage', Hardy makes himself the almost comic victim of his awareness of the mind's tendency to patterned stiffness, playing at his own expense with the 'interaction between seeing and knowing and expecting'. His own experience of the places he visits—of 'Genova the Proud', of Fiesole or of the Palatine or of the Vatican—is, before he actually tests his vision with sight, purely imaginative, and, when he is about to confront the thing itself, his imagining is converted to expectation. In these poems, Hardy corrects his own, often heroic, vision with his own, most usually expressly unheroic, observation. In 'Rome: Building of a New Street in the Ancient Quarters' (69), he sets layers of time against one another in images of descending degrees of hardness and in patterns of diminishing firmness of shape. The crumbling architectural forms embody an idea of time's destructiveness, of course, but they also point to the workmen who 'within these ruins' very shade' are already creating a new shape against disorder. In spite of Hardy's return to grand utterance in the last two lines, it is the singing workmen who are his poem's most vivid sight. In 'The Old Theatre, Fiesole' (67), the poet's perspective is suddenly enlarged by a child who shows him an ancient coin and makes him aware of meanings he had failed to see:

> As with one half blind
> Whom common simples cure, her act flashed home
> In that mute moment to my opened mind
> The power, the pride, the reach of perished Rome.

And in the charming 'Genoa and the Mediterranean' (65), Hardy mocks himself for clinging to an idea of classical perfection. He sees the 'epic-famed, god-haunted Central Sea' and 'Genova the Proud' not in their classical purity, but across a line of 'fishwives' high-hung smocks'. His inflated language is full of self-irony: 'I first beheld thee clad', he apologizes, 'not as the Beauty but the Dowd':

> Out from a deep-delved way my vision lit
> On housebacks pink, green, ochreous—where a slit
> Shoreward 'twixt row and row revealed the classic
>   blue through it.

And thereacross waved fishwives' high-hung smocks,
Chrome kerchiefs, scarlet hose, darned underfrocks;
Often since when my dreams of thee, O Queen, that frippery
mocks:

Whereat I grieve, Superba!

In his delighted deflation of his expectation of a perfect, classical
beauty, and his mock-apology for the ragged 'frippery' of the
living city, Hardy scores a comic point against himself for his
closed, protected vision. 'But, Queen,' he concludes,

such squalid undress none should see,
Those dream-endangering eyewounds no more be
Where lovers first behold thy form in pilgrimage to thee.

In all of these poems, Hardy submits experience to reconsideration. In most of them, he opposes the mind's 'formalization'
of past experience, or its merely conventional expectations, to the
'fresh originality of living fact', shattering pattern in the presentation of an unexpected object—an aged lover, an ancient coin,
a washing line hung with scarlet hose. In some poems, however,
Hardy shows a movement in the other direction, placing before
us an object or dramatic event which, returning, he makes into
an element of pattern.

In 'A Commonplace Day' (78), 'The Contretemps' (539) and
'The Convergence of the Twain' (248), Hardy shows the order-
hungry mind stylizing its experience. Each of these poems breaks
into two, pivoting on a single word from a description in vivid
particulars of an object or event to an abstract or figurative
description of the same thing. The first half of 'A Commonplace
Day', for instance, reports the end of a day which will 'join the
anonymous host / Of those that throng oblivion'. Hardy presents
the day's end in mere, brilliant particulars:

I part the fire-gnawed logs,
Rake forth the embers, spoil the busy flames, and lay the ends
Upon the shining dogs;
Further and further from the nooks the twilight's stride extends,
And beamless black impends.

The lines perfectly exemplify the point of the poem's first half:
the day on which 'Nothing of tiniest worth' was achieved has

only the value of its existence, now ending. But that thought awakens Hardy's 'regret', and on the repetition of that word he turns to consider what might have been the more than particular value of the day. His consideration transforms into metaphor the sensory particulars of the lines quoted above:

> —Yet, maybe, in some soul,
> In some spot undiscerned on sea or land, some impulse rose,
> Or some intent upstole
> Of that enkindling ardency from whose maturer glows
> The world's amendment flows . . . .

'The Contretemps' (539), whose first five stanzas manage a plot of extreme, absurd complication, demonstrates a similar shift from particulars to pattern. It opens with an exquisite series of blunders: the speaker of the poem, rushing to an assignation, accidentally embraces a woman who, rushing to an assignation (but not with him) accidentally embraces him and so loses her husband and her lover, both of whom have observed the action and supposed themselves betrayed. The complications exemplify the chaos of an unplanned world, as is their purpose, and Hardy confirms his purpose in his imagery. The embrace itself is picked out of surrounding darkness by a 'lamp in the gloom'; and the vague air of a 'thawing brume' allows only the close-up details to be seen. The scene (one character is said to 'enter') is a 'lamplit, snowflaked, sloppiness'. The perspective is extremely narrow; the light prevents anything but the object from occupying the fovea.[18] In the sixth stanza, however, the poem draws back, unfolds an increasingly long view of the events it has presented. Its speaker becomes inward and accounts for his actions. His account transforms accident into romance, sloppiness into aesthetic shape:

> So it began; and I was young,
> She pretty, by the lamp,
> As flakes came waltzing down among
> The waves of her clinging hair, that hung
> Heavily on her temples, dark and damp.

As the 'twain hearts caught in one catastrophe' wonder what to do, Hardy slides them a step farther into fantasy, voicing their desire in the noise of the Jersey boat: ' "One pairing is as good as another / Where all is venture! Take each other, / And scrap the oaths that you have aforetime made."' By the end of the poem, the incident of dramatic particulars has become illustrative, remote, an example of the general truth that 'Happiness comes in full to none'.

Like 'The Contretemps', 'The Convergence of the Twain' balances its two halves on the word, 'Well'. The word occurs in the sixth stanza:

> Well: while was fashioning
> This creature of cleaving wing,
> The Immanent Will that stirs and urges everything

VII

> Prepared a sinister mate
> For her—so gaily great—
> A Shape of Ice, for the time far and dissociate.

Unlike most of Hardy's poems, 'The Convergence of the Twain' is personless: the questing mind is explicitly excluded; the speaking voice is never personal. The shift in the middle of the poem, a brilliant chronological and stylistic leap, sets the elements of Hardy's central conflict into a kind of pure antithesis. On one side of his pivotal word, Hardy gives an account of the Titanic as object, remote from the 'Pride of Life that planned her', wrenched out of place in any design or pattern. Matter which had its sense in relation to mind is now mere matter, observed in its slow sea-changes by the 'sea-worm' and the 'Dim, moon-eyed fishes'. In the second half of the poem, Hardy submits that mere material to order. Reaching backwards in time, he finds the pattern of which the *Titanic's* wreck is an item. She becomes now a part of the blind figure in the mind of the Immanent Will. Reporting pattern, Hardy shifts his style, transforms the direct, sensory language of the poem's first half into the figurative pattern of its second half. The sexual metaphor which is suggested in the sixth stanza is the poem's principle of organization by the seventh, racing to the end. After the pivotal 'Well' in this poem there is nothing *but* order.

'The Convergence of the Twain' perfects Hardy's irony. It sets mere object against mere pattern, dismantles the recurring conflict of his poems, and shows 'the sensuous mind' abused. In this poem, which is less about convergence than the division of matter from mind, Hardy excludes consciousness, blinds the mortal eye. Most of his poems make consciousness central: in them, the sensuous mind lives by preserving its conflicts, by repeatedly submitting its formalizations to correction in the fire of sensory apprehension.

NOTES

1. *Personal Writings*, ed. Harold Orel (1967), pp. 36, 37.
2. *Ibid.*, p. 31.
3. *Ibid.*, p. 22.
4. Cf. Barbara Hardy, '*Under the Greenwood Tree*: A Novel about the Imagination' in Anne Smith, ed., *The Novels of Thomas Hardy* (1979), pp. 45–57.
5. Yeats, *Autobiographies* (1966), p. 83.
6. E.g., *CP*, p. 557.
7. Yeats, *Autobiographies*, p. 125.
8. *CP*, p. [84].
9. *CP*, pp. 561–62.
10. *CP*, p. [190].
11. E. H. Gombrich, *The Sense of Order, A Study in the Psychology of Decorative Art* (Oxford, 1979), p. 99. (My title is a deformation of a phrase from this book.)
12. T. S. Eliot, *Collected Plays* (1962), p. 135.
13. *The Sense of Order*, p. 151.
14. *Ibid.*
15. *Wessex Poems* (1898), p. 177.
16. Paul Zietlow, *Moments of Vision* (Cambridge, 1974), p. 159.
17. T. S. Eliot, *Selected Essays* (1932; repr. 1972), p. 300.
18. Cf. T. S. Eliot, 'Reflections on Contemporary Poetry', *The Egoist,* IV.9 (Oct. 1917), p. 133.

10

Travelling Man

by SIMON GATRELL

> I pace along, the rain-shafts riddling me,
> Mile after mile out by the moorland way,
> And up the hill, and through the ewe-leaze gray
> Into the lane, and round the corner tree;
>
> Where, as my clothing clams me, mire-bestarred,
> And the enfeebled light dies out of day,
> Leaving the liquid shades to reign, I say,
> 'This is a hardship to be calendared!'
>
> Yet sires of mine now perished and forgot,
> When worse beset, ere roads were shapen here,
> And night and storm were foes indeed to fear,
> Times numberless have trudged across this spot
> In sturdy muteness on their strenuous lot,
> And taking all such toils as trifles mere.
>   'A Wet Night' (229)

For the narrator of this sonnet the journey outlined in the first quatrain is one so frequently made that its stages require no definition beyond 'the moorland way', 'the hill', 'the lane'. The journey is not taken for pleasure, and Hardy makes us sufficiently aware of its discomfort; but in the sestet the narrator withdraws along the axis of time, to offer the past perspective of his ancestors all making the same journey in even harder conditions. The historical continuity is satisfying, and the poem stresses an essential part of existence—arduous, unpleasurable, but una-voidable. This idea colours a whole range of Hardy's poetry: often the journey is implied, unemphasised, neither hard nor easy, simply part of the background; but in a large number of poems the travelling is central.

Hardy's idea of the journey offers a field in which a number of important elements in his verse can flourish. Walking, the most usual form of his journeying, leads to an active and intimate contact with the environment and so can serve as the frame of his observations, and, in addition to poems which describe this contact directly, there are many, like 'The Darkling Thrush' (119), in which the reader understands that the narrator experienced the moment described while abroad on a journey. Travelling is also an integral part of pilgrimage, an activity strongly present to Hardy's imagination before the death of his first wife, Emma, and increasingly so thereafter. Journeying.is, furthermore, a ready metaphor for life, and Hardy explores its possibilities fully. Finally, the inevitable chance encounters of travelling facilitate one of Hardy's characteristic activities as a poet, the infilling of other existences with that of his narrator. From the rounds of the Quire in *Under the Greenwood Tree* to Tess Durbeyfield's wanderings across the length and breadth of South Wessex, journeying is of singular importance in Hardy's fiction, not a feature of his narratives that he hastened over as a necessary plot mechanism, but one that he dwelt on and elaborated, incorporated into the thematic patterns of the novels. So it is also with his poetry.

It may seem perverse to begin my discussion with almost the only poem that makes deliberate use of the lack of a journey, but 'Wessex Heights' (261), which has recently been used to illustrate critical versions of Hardy as a poet, suggests the central place of the idea in Hardy's mind. The major part of the poem describes not the Heights themselves, but the country below, from which the narrator escapes on the Heights. One feature of this lowland life, though not the most immediately arresting, is its restless or impeded travel—'I am tracked by phantoms', 'I cannot go', 'one in the railway train'—while, on the hilltops, 'men have never cared to haunt, nor women walked with me'. We are given no knowledge whatever of how the narrator reaches the Heights—the phrases Hardy uses are 'when I stand, / Say, on Ingpen Beacon ...' in the first verse, and 'So I am found on Ingpen Beacon ...' in the last. No other poem of Hardy's combines such attention to topographical detail with a total absence of journeying to reach the named goals. It gives a sense almost of a magical appearance—at one moment the space at the summit of the hill is empty, at the next it is filled with Hardy's narrator escaping the ghosts that haunt his movements in the valleys below.

It is interesting to compare 'Wessex Heights' with 'He Follows Himself' (604), which shares a similar underlying conception, that of the self watching the self: 'In a heavy time I dogged myself / Along a louring way . . . .' Here Hardy uses not place-names, but metaphors for the grave he is visiting, and he emphasises the labour that is required to reach it. This poem, like 'Wessex Heights', shows the narrator needing escape from himself as much as from other haunting spirits.

The Heights offer the feeling of almost boundless space and of effortlessness in attaining them; though apparently anchored by their 'real' names, they seem insubstantial, like the palaces of Prospero's vision. The narrator 'found' on Ingpen Beacon and the rest, when compared with the intensely physical 'I' and 'myself' in 'He Follows Himself', seems almost disembodied: 'I seem where I was before my birth, and after death may be . . . .'

It is the life in the valleys beneath the Heights that is Hardy's more general concern, and in 'An Autumn Rain-Scene' (569), he embodies all the variety of the life down there in an expansion of the single journey in the octave of 'A Wet Night' (229). He was also aware that journeying was for some not just a daily task, but a way of life. 'Christmastide' (829), for instance, contrasts the narrator—a benighted walker in conditions and mood very similar to those of the narrator in 'A Wet Night'—with 'a sodden tramp', whose 'cheerful voice called, nigh me, / "A merry Christmas, friend!" ', and who

> breaking
> Into thin song, bore straight
> Ahead, direction taking
> Toward the Casuals' gate.

The response to the poem is complex because of Hardy's restraint in not drawing out the implications of the encounter, but leaving the reader to consider the two attitudes towards the night, and then to go further and visualise the welcome awaiting the sodden tramp when he reaches the Casuals' gate.

'A Trampwoman's Tragedy' (153), the greatest of the poems that centre on walking as a way of life, might be divided into three sections. The first describes the life of the group tramping round Wessex; it uses verbs like 'We beat afoot', 'We jaunted on', 'we had padded side by side', and makes the road seem, on the surface at least, as jolly as it was for the Christmastide tramp, sufficiently so to overcome 'sun-blaze', 'toilsome Poldon crest' and 'every Marshwood midge'. But in the fifth verse the verb of motion changes tone as the narrator turns to her particular story—'Now as we trudged—O deadly day'—and the ballad-swift tale of jealousy and murder ensues. At the ninth verse she turns to the present, and the verbs again change tone, to the simple, 'I walked the world alone', and finally 'here alone I stray', bereft of purpose and motive. We see freedom from social restraint followed by the imposition of the ultimate social retribution, companionship succeeded by desolate loneliness, embodied in contrasted journeyings.

This poem also enforces the contrast between 'Wessex Heights' and the majority of Hardy's poems, for as the narrator in 'Wessex Heights' defines the limits of his environment by naming the bordering hills that offer him sanctuary, so the narrator in this poem defines hers by naming the 'Lone inns we loved'. This narrator, however, emphasises contact with the land trodden over and the effort needed to attain these wayside taps.

Pilgrimage, or travelling in response to an inner compulsion, drew Hardy even more than did functional journeys. It is almost always love or a related emotion which drives the pilgrims to their road, towards a shrine of some kind. Pilgrimage may be presented without narrative, as in the delightful small song, 'If It's Ever Spring Again' (548):

> If it's ever spring again,
>   Spring again,
> I shall go where went I when
> Down the moor-cock splashed, and hen,
> Seeing me not, amid their flounder,
> Standing with my arm around her;
> If it's ever spring again,
>   Spring again,
> I shall go where went I then.

More typically, Hardy's pilgrimages are narratives of travel. 'The Nettles' (469) depends upon the pathos of contrast between the labour of the mother's journey to her son's grave and the proximity to it of his widow's house, and upon the stoicism of the mother emphasised by the broken rhythm of 'It is enough. I'll turn and go'. The feel of the poem is very much like that in the crucial chapter of *The Return of the Native* where Mrs. Yeobright turns away from Clym's house after apparently being refused admittance by Eustacia. It is characteristic of Hardy's pilgrimage that it offers no release or satisfaction.

Two relatively early poems, 'The Supplanter' (142) and 'The Revisitation' (152) complicate the same basic idea with other interests. 'The Supplanter' begins with a customarily arduous journey:

> He bends his travel-tarnished feet
>   To where she wastes in clay:
> From day-dawn until eve he fares
>   Along the wintry way;
> From day-dawn until eve he bears
>   A wreath of blooms and bay.

The narrative has much of the spareness and some of the diction of the traditional ballad. The pilgrim is invited to the birthday party of the daughter of the Keeper of the Field of Tombs, spends the night with her, and is seduced from his purpose. In the morning his remorse is fierce:

> 'Now could I kill thee here!' he says,
>   'For winning me from one
> Who ever in her living days
>   Was pure as cloistered nun!'

and he disappears in ballad-fashion nowhere in particular ('and, rising, roves he then / Afar for many a mile') until a year later, in a variation of the first stanza, he returns to the graveyard to make amends to his dead love's memory. The daughter is there 'outcast, shamed, and bare' with their child:

> He turns—unpitying, passion-tossed;
>   'I know you not!' he cries,
> 'Nor know your child. I knew this maid,
>   But she's in Paradise!'
> And he has vanished in the shade
>   From her beseeching eyes.

The historic present of the last lines is another characteristic of the ballad, as is the bitter cruelty. Our response to this poem is ambiguous; the seduction of the pilgrim is made to seem sordid—spirits of dead loved ones are strong magic in Hardy, and the pilgrim sees that of his beloved immediately before succumbing to the daughter. Yet the pilgrim's rejection of his child and its mother seems intolerably harsh. What is clear is that the emotion which stimulated the pilgrimage in the first place is much stronger than the counter-emotion by which it is seduced for a single night; though the question whether love for the dead is better than lust with the living is perhaps hardly answerable in the context of the poem, and the shock of pain is what most strongly abides.

In 'The Revisitation' the pilgrim is a soldier, inspired by a coincidence of dates and places to make the short journey to the place where he and his beloved had parted twenty years before. This journey is described in terms very different from the pilgrimage in 'The Supplanter'. The poem emphasises the atmosphere rather than the effort of the journey, and instead of ballad-brevity and anonymity, it gives a long description full of environmental detail. The accompaniments of the journey are ominous, the landscape threatening, but the whimsical pilgrimage appears to develop satisfactorily when the soldier's former love suddenly turns up. Still as far away from ballad convention as possible, Hardy is concerned with the probability of her appearance:

> 'Twas not reasonless: below there
> In the vale, had been her home; the nook might hold her even
> yet . . . .

They meet, talk, and renew their love in the darkness, imagining that there had been 'a signal-thrill' between them to bring them thus together; he falls asleep. When he wakes it is to a glorious sunrise and a 'spacious landscape', but just as the uneasy forebodings of the night had not fulfilled themselves, so now the glory surrounding them mocks the lovers, the light revealing the effect on her face of that favourite of Hardyan tools, 'Time's transforming chisel'. She catches his look of dismay and 'With the too proud temper ruling that had parted us before' she leaves him. He does not follow, but 'Soon I bent my footsteps townward, /

Like to one who had watched a crime.' It is characteristic of
Hardy that while a momentary union with the beloved is possibly
joyful, extension of that moment is bound to bring disillusion:
the achieving of the pilgrimage—the double pilgrimage—in the
meeting not of memories or of spirits, but of the former lovers
themselves, can only succeed temporarily, under cover of darkness.
When Agnette says, with emphasis, 'It is *just* as ere we parted!',
she is right, though beyond her intended meaning, for if her joy
is the same, so is her pride, and we may well imagine that their
previous parting had been very similar.

'A Last Journey' (685) is another variation on the theme of
pilgrimage. A dying father tells his daughter of the dream he has
had:

> The whole night have I footed field and turnpike-way—
> A regular pilgrimage—as at my best
> And very briskest day!

He relates the sequence of visits he made with such circumstantial
vividness that on being told the next day that her father has died,
the girl asks

> That journey, then, did father really go?—
> Buy nuts, and cakes, and travel at night till dawn was red,
> And tire himself with journeying, as he said,
> To see those old friends that he cared for so?

The dream-journey has the same reality for both dying man and
child, and the reader too enters that reality.

None of these poems is autobiographical, unlike the familiar
series based upon the two journeys which Hardy actually made
to North Cornwall, the one on which he met his future wife,
Emma, and the one he made after her death. A fragment from
'After a Journey' (289) expresses the purpose of his pilgrimage
of love-remorse:

> Yes: I have re-entered your olden haunts at last;
> Through the years, through the dead scenes I have tracked
> you.

It is not coincidental that those poems most generally acknowledged to be the best of the section subtitled *Veteris Vestigia
Flammae* are those specifically connected with this or another

pilgrimage, as in 'The Voice' (285). The only exception is 'The
Going' (277), a poem in which the very title implies a journey,
and in which the implied journey gives a chilling and moving
dimension to the figure of pilgrimage in the poems which follow.
This poem, which stands first in the group, also names the scene
of the pilgrimage, 'those red-veined rocks far West'. These poems
fuse Hardy's most intense perception of emotion, environment,
and the sought spirit of the dead.

This union makes 'At Castle Boterel' (292) at once one of
Hardy's greatest poems, and one that seems most typical of him
as a writer. The road and its surrounds are the material in which
the power of emotion has etched a permanent sign, one of such
strength that the spirit of the girl who was the cause of that
emotion remains on the spot to be perceived by those who have
eyes to see. It is the pilgrim who sees, who brings again into
being the phantom figure, who preserves her immortality. Without the journey to the spot, the figure—that figure—could not
exist, though the place itself, the 'primaeval rocks', store the
energy that creates the phantom.

His pilgrimage after Emma's death also encouraged Hardy to
recall and write about his first journey to St. Juliot in 1870. At
least four poems relate directly to this trip, each written from a
different perspective, and it is instructive to consider them as a
group. Of the two published in the same volume as *Veteris
Vestigia Flammae* one is the most celebrated, 'When I Set Out
for Lyonnesse' (254), and the other is 'The Discovery' (271).
There is one more in each of the next two collections, 'The
Wind's Prophecy' (440) and 'A Man Was Drawing Near to Me'
(536). These poems have other elements in common besides their
subject: three employ a repetitive structure with incremental
effect, depending on variation within a given verbal as well as
stanzaic pattern for the satisfaction it offers; each takes up with
varying intensity the element of mystery that in retrospect seemed
to surround the journey.

The latest published of these poems is seen from Emma's point
of view; it contrasts the static, unprepared narrator with the man
as we trace him nearer to her, moving in space and time through
each verse, from Halworthy, through Otterham, past Tresparret
Posts, by Hennet Byre to her door. We are alternately with the
narrator and with the man, sensing the narrowing gap between

them as the stanzas are completed, until the climax arrives:

> There was a rumble at the door,
> A draught disturbed the drapery,
> And but a minute passed before,
>> With gaze that bore
>> My destiny,
> The man revealed himself to me.

The sequel, whether of good or evil portent, is left unsaid. The movement of the poem is very like that in 'The Convergence of the Twain' (248), which describes the sinking of the Titanic (itself, of course, bound on a journey). The sense of mystery, of ignorance in the mutual approach, is very strong there too:

IX

> Alien they seemed to be:
> No mortal eye could see
> The intimate welding of their later history.

X

> Or sign that they were bent
> By paths coincident
> On being anon twin halves of one august event,

XI

> Till the Spinner of the Years
> Said 'Now!' And each one hears,
> And consummation comes, and jars two hemispheres.

In 'The Wind's Prophecy' repetitive formality is not so satisfying; the first four lines of each verse describe the threatening landscape, ominous and fierce, through which the man is travelling; in the second four he speaks his conviction that he is leaving his love behind him, while the howling wind claims that on the contrary she lies before him. The landscape description is often strained, and the two voices come to no conclusion. Of course biography can fill in more detail, provide us with the knowledge that the wind was right, but the underlying weakness remains in the forced anthropomorphism of the wind's words. It is never clear whether the traveller hears the wind's words himself, for he never engages with it, as it does with him.

The theme of ignorance is again central in 'The Discovery', a two-stanza poem founded not upon an incremental structure, but upon a contrast. The first stanza is again ominous—'crude coast', 'funeral pyres', 'distant cannonades that set the land shaking'—but more satisfying than in 'The Wind's Prophecy', because the images are compressed into a single impression instead of diffused through a long poem. The first line of the second verse provides the fulcrum ('And so I never once guessed') that turns the poem from the threatening of doom to the promise of 'A Love-nest, / Bowered and candle-lit', and leads to the energetic, joyful, 'Where I burst on her my heart could not but follow'. 'Burst' brings the stanza back to the implications of the unexpected with which it opens.

In 'When I Set Out for Lyonnesse' the unexpected is intensified into the magical—

> Nor did the wisest wizard guess
> What would bechance at Lyonnesse
> While I should sojourn there.
>
> When I came back from Lyonnesse
> With magic in my eyes . . .

—while the journey itself, so much the centre of the other poems, vanishes into a distance—a hundred miles—and a couple of romantic environmental details: 'The rime was on the spray, / And starlight lit my lonesomeness . . . . ' This single journey had a specially vivid place in Hardy's memory after his wife's death. His astonishing virtuosity created from it four separate poems, with similar patterns and the similar dominant theme of surprise and fateful discovery, that are yet so different in the effects they achieve.

Hardy may have felt that 'When I Set Out for Lyonnesse' was too full of joy, and so later countered it in 'I Rose and Went to Rou'tor Town' (468). The titles of both poems are derived from their first lines; both concern journeys to fictionally named Cornish places; the verse forms are similar, the only major difference being the failure to repeat the first line as the fifth of the first verse of 'Rou'tor Town'; both have three stanzas; both employ the unusual word *sojourn*. In this case, however, it is the woman who speaks:

> I rose and went to Rou'tor Town
>   With gaiety and good heart,
>   And ardour for the start,
> That morning ere the moon was down
> That lit me off to Rou'tor Town
>   With gaiety and good heart.
>
> When sojourn soon at Rou'tor Town
>   Wrote sorrows on my face,
>   I strove that none should trace
> The pale and gray, once pink and brown,
> When sojourn soon at Rou'tor Town
>   Wrote sorrows on my face.
>
> The evil wrought at Rou'tor Town
>   On him I'd loved so true
>   I cannot tell anew:
> But naught can quench, but naught can drown
> The evil wrought at Rou'tor Town
>   On him I'd loved so true!

This poem may be Hardy's attempt to recast 'Lyonnesse' in tragic terms, to see whether the method of suggesting joy through understatement and the judicious use of a few appropriately charged words could also be applied to foreboding and pain. I do not think he succeeded.

In most of the travelling poems the narrator is himself the journeyer, but there are some in which the narrator is static and the travelling is being done by those he observes; this situation offers possibilities for a variety of viewpoints, and a number of poems published in *Human Shows* suggest that Hardy was consciously experimenting in this mode. The most simple is 'Nobody Comes' (715), with its first-person narrator solidly established by the last lines of the poem: 'And mute by the gate I stand again alone / And nobody pulls up there.' It is chiefly memorable for the imaginative use Hardy makes of the self-enclosed speed of the motor-car and the pool of its headlamps to intensify the isolation of the man standing watching the road.

In 'Shortening Days at the Homestead' (791), though the narrator does not introduce himself into the poem, we are conscious of his presence as he notes the details of his environment that speak of autumn. The narrator and the poet are in harmony; the composite picture is dynamic but unemphatic, complete despite its brevity. 'A Light Snow-Fall after Frost' (702) is slightly more complicated. For the first three verses we seem, as in 'Shortening Days', to be in the companionship of an observant and imaginative person viewing the world through his window-pane; he is comfortable, warm and perhaps rather bored ('On the flat road a man *at last* appears'—my emphasis). The comparison between the second traveller and the holly trees belongs to this observant, bored narrator. But then in the fourth verse—

> The snow-feathers so gently swoop that though
>   But half an hour ago
> The road was brown, and now is starkly white,
> A watcher would have failed defining quite
>   When it transformed it so

—we are unnerved by the sudden impersonality of 'a watcher'; the narrator trying to persuade us, it seems, that he has not been watching the road himself for the last half-hour. He withdraws from responsibility, and leaves us wondering where we stand both in relation to what we have been shown and in relation to him.

'Life and Death at Sunrise' (698) more openly separates the poet and the narrator. In the three previous poems the reader has no difficulty in accepting that he is in company with the narrator watching an actual scene, listening to his interpretation of it; indeed, it is this ready acceptance which makes the last two lines of 'A Light Snow-Fall' so arresting. But here even the subtitle ('Near Dogbury Gate 1867') has elements of artifice: it is intended to assure us of the actuality of the meeting, but by the end of the poem the reader is doing a little elementary maths to assure himself that Hardy has got the dates right—ah yes, if he were ninety in 1867 John Thinn would have been twelve in 1789. That the baby is to be called Jack and the corpse was John is a coincidence that might be overlooked in Hardy's fiction, but is more noticeable in the poetry. There is fine artistry in the suspension of the dawn chorus and accompanying cacophony until the creak of the waggon and the clip of the horse's hooves have echoed to the reader through apparent silence, and also in the organisation of the time—the meeting of night and day—and the place—half-way up (or down) the hill—so that the moment is seen as poised between absolutes, as are the two principal participants. The poem's reminiscence of *A Winter's Tale* ('thou mettest with things dying, I with things new-born') is striking.

It is paradoxical that Hardy wished to be thought of as a faithful observer and recorder, and yet so clearly believed in the subjective nature of each individual's response to everything outside him. 'The King's Experiment' (132) perfectly exemplifies his belief: a man travels in the rain to visit his love singing of fair skies, discovers that she is dead, and returns in the sunshine, murmuring of horizons hung with gloom. As King Doom says to Dame Nature (these two having arranged the circumstances of the journey as an experiment):

> And there's the humour, as I said;
> Thy dreary dawn he saw as gleaming gold,
> And in thy glistening green and radiant red
> Funereal gloom and cold.

When Hardy's poems relate human encounters, the conflict between subjective and objective becomes more disturbing. That a man and a boy in 'Midnight on the Great Western' (465) are sitting in the same carriage facing each other is beyond doubt, and the scene is vividly before us; but throughout, despite the attention paid to the boy, it is the narrator of whom we are conscious. It is he who suggests the boy is 'bewrapt past knowing to what he was going, / Or whence he came'; it is he who sees the lamp's beams as sad, he who enters the boy's consciousness, making him like Little Father Time, and who in the end exalts him, as another of Hardy's narrators does an old thrush. We are offered an objective encounter, which we accept, and a rising crescendo of subjective interpretation which tells us much about the narrator, but almost nothing about the boy.

'Coming Up Oxford Street: Evening' (684) offers a similar situation in a more distinct form. The first verse is purely observation, describing the effects of sunlight in the street; and the second, distinguished from the first by metre, begins with more observation until the third line when with something of a start we are shifted into a city-clerk's consciousness. Is this clerk the observer himself under a mask of third-person anonymity, or is the narrator going beyond observation and interpreting the visage of the clerk as he passes? The footnote 'As seen July 4, 1872' suggests the latter explanation, in which case the flood of gloom after the neutral description is highly disturbing.

It is interesting to compare with these ambiguous and disturbing poems one which instead of setting up a contrast between neutral observation and subjective interpretation, reconciles them. In 'Beyond the Last Lamp' (257) the pair who 'seemed lovers' are held at a slight distance; the first-person narrator's penetration of them is less specific than in the other poems; their objective actions support his interpretation; and above all the focus upon the response of the narrator to the scene allows the mingling of observation and interpretation to be subsumed into a greater passion:

> There they seem brooding on their pain,
> And will, while such a lane remain.

It is another expression of Hardy's doctrine of spirits, linked in its intensity to 'At Castle Boterel'. The couple achieve an immortality in the narrator's eyes not unlike that which the nightingale possessed for Keats.

The idea of the journey too takes on a kind of immortality when Hardy uses it as a metaphor for life; this can be seen at its most straightforward in 'The Weary Walker' (713). The continual recurrence of 'the road' leads to a fascination in the eye and ear of the reader with the shape and sound of the words, which begin by the end of the poem to lose their distinctive value as counters of meaning and become hypnotic forms and murmurs, much as the eternal presence for the walker of the shape of the road before him and the sound of it beneath his feet would become hypnotic—even though the alternating rhyme-words offer glances around at the 'wide country'.

Occasionally Hardy narrows down the application of the metaphor to a smaller stretch of the road of life. 'A Wasted Illness' (122) images the end of the road as a terrifying cavern leading to 'the all-delivering door'. The narrator treads the path until, in sight of the door, he recovers; the door fades, 'And back slid I / Along the galleries by which I came', until he reaches the tract of open country where life is lived, and 'I roam anew'.

His regret, however, is that 'those grim chambers, must be ranged again / To reach that door.'

The finest of the poems that use the life-as-a-journey metaphor is 'The Five Students' (439):

> The sparrow dips in his wheel-rut bath,
>   The sun grows passionate-eyed,
> And boils the dew to smoke by the paddock-path;
>   As strenuously we stride,—
> Five of us; dark He, fair He, dark She, fair She, I,
>   All beating by.
>
> The air is shaken, the high-road hot,
>   Shadowless swoons the day,
> The greens are sobered and cattle at rest; but not
>   We on our urgent way,—
> Four of us; fair She, dark She, fair He, I, are there,
>   But one—elsewhere.
>
> Autumn moulds the hard fruit mellow,
>   And forward still we press
> Through moors, briar-meshed plantations, clay-pits yellow
>   As in the spring hours—yes,
> Three of us; fair He, fair She, I, as heretofore,
>   But—fallen one more.
>
> The leaf drops: earthworms draw it in
>   At night-time noiselessly,
> The fingers of birch and beech are skeleton-thin
>   And yet on the beat are we,—
> Two of us; fair She, I. But no more left to go
>   The track we know.
>
> Icicles tag the church-aisle leads,
>   The flag-rope gibbers hoarse,
> The home-bound foot-folk wrap their snow-flaked heads,
>   Yet I still stalk the course—
> One of us . . . Dark and fair He, dark and fair She, gone:
>   The rest—anon.

This has the repetitive framework of many of Hardy's most successful poems, with an incremental effect derived, perhaps, from the traditional ballads; and here the effects are carefully managed. The track metaphor is given heightened reality by the vividness of the accompanying landscape, the intense particularity of the observation: the sparrow's dusty bath, the mellow-moulding of the fruit, the silence of the earthworm. There is considerable satisfaction in the completion of the double movement of the poem, the diminishment of the travelling companions and the progression of the seasons of the year. The seasons are revivified as metaphors for the stages of life by the energy of Hardy's images, that have the virtue of being detailed and generalised at the same time. He has taken the same care in the gradations in the movement along the road: 'strenuously we stride'; 'on our urgent way'; 'forward still we press'; 'yet on the beat are we'; 'I still stalk the course'—the pace ever slackens as the seasons draw on. This is Hardy's fullest use of the journey as a metaphor for life. The metaphor occurs also in a few splendid isolated images, like this from 'After a Journey' (289): 'I am just the same as when / Our days were a joy, and our paths through flowers' or this, from 'The End of the Episode' (178):

> Ache deep; but make no moans:
> Smile out; but stilly suffer:
> The paths of love are rougher
>   Than thoroughfares of stones.

Poems which use travelling as a metaphor for life also have much to do with death, and the destructiveness of time. In 'An Anniversary' (407), which gives a simple contrast between now and then in the same place, 'the same man pilgrims now hereby who pilgrimed here that day', but the man, like the place, is changed for the worse by time. But in another poem about a very similar situation, 'Life Laughs Onward' (394), the narrator travels around searching for places he once knew, but finds that

> Life laughed and moved on unsubdued,
> I saw that Old succumbed to Young:
> 'Twas well. My too regretful mood
>   Died on my tongue.

Hardy, a habitual walker, bicyclist, rider in motor-cars, turned naturally to travel as a way to express most of his characteristic ideas. So did William Barnes, the other great celebrator of the

life of rural Dorset, and it seems right that Hardy's poem in
memory of the elder poet should itself describe the incidents of
a walk. This poem describes a love-journey, for Hardy's reverence
for Barnes is well documented; it is concerned with mortality; in
it Hardy imposes his interpretation on a neutral event; it uses
the landscape to intensify the vision; it even has one of Hardy's
most irritating verbal habits, the use of an adjective and its
comparative together ('hard and harder' in line nine).

412 The Last Signal
(11 Oct., 1886)
A Memory of William Barnes

> Silently I footed by an uphill road
> That led from my abode to a spot yew-boughed;
> Yellowly the sun sloped low down to westward,
> And dark was the east with cloud.
>
> Then, amid the shadow of that livid sad east,
> Where the light was least, and a gate stood wide,
> Something flashed the fire of the sun that was facing it,
> Like a brief blaze on that side.
>
> Looking hard and harder I knew what it meant—
> The sudden shine sent from the livid east scene;
> It meant the west mirrored by the coffin of my friend there,
> Turning to the road from his green,
>
> To take his last journey forth—he who in his prime
> Trudged so many a time from that gate athwart the
> land!
> Thus a farewell to me he signalled on his grave-way,
> As with a wave of his hand.

It is not Barnes's verse that Hardy chose to remember but his
capacity for walking.

11

Read By Moonlight

by JON STALLWORTHY

The longevity of the legend that the reviewers of *Tess* and *Jude* 'killed' Hardy the novelist is remarkable, given the clear evidence in his work that he died by another hand: that of Hardy the poet. When, in 1892, he sat down to write *The Pursuit of the Well-Beloved*, his interest was moving away from the multiple selves peopling the world outside the novelist's window to the single self framed in the mirror shared with his hero, Jocelyn Pierston:

> He was not exactly old, he said to himself the next morning as he beheld his face in the glass. And he looked considerably younger than he was. But there was history in his face—distinct chapters of it; his brow was not the blank page it once had been.
> (pp. 260–61)[1]

The mirror's message was not always so comforting. Another morning, not long afterwards,

> he discerned, a short distance before him, a movement of something ghostly. His position was facing the window, and he found that by chance the looking-glass had swung itself vertical, so that what he saw was his own shape. The recognition startled him. The person he appeared was too grievously far, chronologically, in advance of the person he felt himself to be. (p. 271)

Even had Hardy not admitted to his friend Gosse that he was 'getting old, like Pierston', one would not need to be a lip-reader to recognize the voice given the last word in *Wessex Poems* (1898):

> I look into my glass,
> And view my wasting skin,
> And say, 'Would God it came to pass
> My heart had shrunk as thin!'

Though the title of the 1892 serial version, *The Pursuit of the Well-Beloved*, was shortened to *The Well-Beloved* for the 1897 revision in book form, the sub-title remained unchanged: *A Sketch of a Temperament*. In the way of the more conventional prefatory disclaimer—'Any resemblance to persons living or dead is purely fortuitous'—Hardy's sub-title reminded the world in general, and Mrs. Hardy in particular, that a *Temperament* is not a *Life*. Emma and others close to Pierston's creator cannot have doubted that the temperament was his own, but one hopes they did not detect behind the three incarnations of the Well-Beloved the presence of his three cousins, Rebecca, Martha, and Tryphena Sparks.[2] Be that as it may, on this crypto-autobiographical foundation, Hardy constructed a symbolist novel. Each incarnation of Jocelyn Pierston's Well-Beloved is introduced, attended, reflected, by the moon that is at once her symbol and his own.

The first Avice is invited to walk 'where they could linger and watch the moon rise over the sea. She said she thought she would come' (pp. 22-3). In the event, she changes her mind and Pierston sees her no more until, as 'a young man of forty',

> he looked out of his bedroom window, and began to consider in what direction from where he stood that darling little figure lay. It was straight across there, under the young pale moon. The symbol signified well. The divinity of the silver bow was not more excellently pure than she, the lost, had been. Under that moon was the island of Ancient Slingers, and on the island a house, framed from mullions to chimney-top like the isle itself, of stone. Inside the window, the moonlight irradiating her winding-sheet, lay Avice, reached only by the faint noises inherent in the isle; the tink-tink of the chisels in the quarries, the surging of the tides in the bay. (p. 115)

Pierston sees another vision of her, 'bending over and then withdrawing from her grave in the light of the moon' (p. 122); and, shortly afterwards, meets one who 'was in all respects the Avice he had lost, the girl he had seen in the church-yard and had fancied to be the illusion of a dream' (p. 124).

As 'a young man turned sixty', passing the cottage in which the third Avice had been born, he sees the new moon growing again. In the novel's first, serial version, Hardy's ensuing depiction of Pierston read:

> He was subject to gigantic superstitions. In spite of himself, the sight of the new moon, his chosen tutelary goddess, as representing, by her so-called inconstancy, his own idea of a migratory Well-Beloved, made him start as if his sweetheart in the flesh had suddenly looked over the horizon at him. In a crowd secretly, or in solitude boldly, he had ever bowed the knee three times to this divinity on her first appearance monthly, and directed a soft kiss towards her shining shape. He feared Aphrodite, but Selene he cherished. All this did he, a man of fifty-nine![3]

In his 1897 revision of this passage, the novelist of fifty-seven made a number of significant alterations:

> He was subject to gigantic fantasies still. In spite of himself, the sight of the new moon, as representing one who, by her so-called inconstancy, acted up to his own idea of a migratory Well-Beloved, made him feel as if his wraith, in a changed sex, had suddenly looked over the horizon at him. In a crowd secretly, or in solitude boldly, he had ever bowed the knee three times to this sisterly divinity on her first appearance monthly, and directed a kiss towards her shining shape. (pp. 243–44)

No longer tutelary goddess, representing his sweetheart, the moon is now 'his wraith, in a changed sex', a 'sisterly divinity'. The change marks a shift in Hardy's awareness of the central irony of his novel and his life. As Hillis Miller puts it, in his penetrating Introduction to the New Wessex edition: 'Jocelyn does not really want to join himself to any of the Avices. Such a union would be a kind of incest, and so is subject to a powerful taboo.'

That his narcissism is specifically that of the creative artist emerges more clearly from the opening chapter of the 1892 serial version than from the paragraph into which it was distilled in 1897 (p. 15). The book originally began with Pearston—the spelling of whose name may have been changed to suggest *peer*ing and *pier*-glass rather than *par*ing—burning old love-letters. He desists, however, when he comes upon some whose sentiments 'he had availed himself of in some attempts at lyric verse'; and others by one whose form, 'whose curves as remembered by [him he had] worked into statuettes'.[4] The sculptor believes that he spares the letters out of affection for their authors, whereas it is clearly out of affection for himself as reflected in his own verses and statuettes.

Hardy had great difficulty revising *The Pursuit of the Well-Beloved* and Gittings suggests that this 'shows how weary he had become with prose generally'. Certainly, it is not hard to imagine him weary with this particular tale in 1896; feeling he had not done justice to those 'distinct chapters' of history read in Pierston's mirror; and anxious to explore them in the medium that now seemed more suited to the themes and images obsessing his imagination.

Love betrayed, eclipsed, or suffering—perhaps the central theme of all Hardy's work—is explored in the similar symbolism of one of the *Wessex Poems*, published the year after *The Well-Beloved*. The narrator of 'The Burghers' (23) hears at sunset from a friend that his wife plans to elope 'at the late moon's first gleam' with another man. As he goes to their meeting place, he hears only the River Froom's mild hiss, and the ill omen of moon over water is again fulfilled as the wronged husband watches the lovers' passionate embrace. He cannot bring himself to kill them, but instead takes them home:

> Inside the house none watched; and on we prest
> Before a mirror, in whose gleam I read
> Her beauty, his,—and mine own mien unblest . . . .

The narrator reads the cold message of the mirror; not the lovers who, presumably, have eyes only for each other. At the poem's end, watching their 'moonlit figures' recede, he tells his informer-friend:

> 'I have struck well. They fly,
> But carry wounds that none can cicatrize.'
> —'Not mortal?' said he. 'Lingering—worse,' said I.

The chilling power of 'The Burghers' derives from the fact that the poet admits the reader to the voyeuristic perspective he shares with the husband and the moon. Unable in his sexual inadequacy to share the lovers' ardour, the husband takes comfort—cold but disturbingly evident comfort—in initiating and imagining the corrosive guilt that will cool their ardour to the point where it mirrors his own. Something of the same pattern is repeated in

'A Trampwoman's Tragedy' (153). This again begins with the setting of the sun that is so often in Hardy's poetry a symbol of happiness in love; a symbol less potent than the opposing symbol that presides over the last act of the tragedy:

> The red moon low declined—
> The ghost of him I'd die to kiss
> Rose up and said: 'Ah, tell me this!
> Was the child mine, or was it his?
>   Speak, that I rest may find!'

Hearing that there were no grounds for his jealousy, murder, and execution, the ghost 'smiled, and thinned away', leaving his former love herself to 'haunt' the moor, and the moon to contemplate a completed circuit as frigid as her own.

As if aware of the gorgon gaze of his moon's-eye view, Hardy's first poetic response to finding himself caught in its beam was to write 'Shut Out That Moon' (164):

> Close up the casement, draw the blind,
>   Shut out that stealing moon . . . .

Casement and window are important symbols in his work, in that they offer both a perspective outward or inward and a barrier between the perceiver and object of perception. Here, the poet asks a listener (presumably Emma) to put that barrier and the blind between them and the moon, which will otherwise steal in and, he implies, steal more than she has already stolen: love songs played on 'our lutes' and those to whom they were played. The speaker's request is, of course, too late. The moonlight is already in the room, making chilling contrast between now and then, tart fruit and early bloom. Even so, the poet begs pathetically that his 'eyes and thought' be imprisoned in the room where the lamp, rather than the moon, presides; the mechanic lamp by whose 'common' light he makes the 'mechanic speech' that is all he has to offer his listener/reader now that the singing lute is stilled. Narcissus, the voyeur, is doomed to watch himself reflected in his own cold page.

In 'The Division' (169) there is rain rather than moonlight on the windows,

> But that thwart thing betwixt us twain,
>   Which nothing cleaves or clears,
> Is more than distance, Dear, or rain,
>   And longer than the years!

Perennial subject and metaphor, image and reflection, are reversed in a poem that picks up two key words from that stanza, 'The Convergence of the Twain' (248). The feminine ship, her fires extinguished, 'couches' in solitude (and one thinks of Emma, only a few months from death, at Max Gate). The prying eye of the poet picks out her mirror and jewels, their bright expectations unfulfilled. That unfulfilment is expressed in revealingly human terms: the mirrors 'glass' only the *dumb* sea-worm and the jewels are *blind*. All this is seen by the 'moon-eyed fishes' which, in the necessary absence of the moon, embody the narrator's detached imagination, and into whose mouths is put the question he must answer:

> 'What does this vaingloriousness down here?' . . .

VI

> Well: while was fashioning
> This creature of cleaving wing,
> The Immanent Will that stirs and urges everything

VII

> Prepared a sinister mate
> For her—so gaily great—
> A Shape of Ice, for the time far and dissociate.

Hardy's moon's-eye view, his wraith's perspective, leaves him free to play his leading role in his own poems: here, the Shape of Ice destined to 'mate' with the hot-hearted ship. While she is 'fashioning'—a verb beautifully in accord with the other feminine terms by which she is described—the iceberg simply grows, unnoticed by the world and not described by the poet. 'Alien they seemed to be': but the Spinner of the Years, having arranged this marriage of fire and ice, knows better. In a grim parody of the platonic symbol of perfection, the 'twin halves' are brought to their 'intimate welding'—a phrase that is itself a brilliant welding/wédding of the poem's subject and metaphor, the sensuous and the technological. The consummation of iceberg and vessel, the one piercing the other below the water-line, is at once a sexual consummation and a violent ending that calls to mind Christ's last words from the cross: '*Consummatum est*'. 'It is finished.' For 'the smart ship', marriage meant death as the iceberg quenched her fires. Coldness has begotten coldness. The frigid circuit is again complete.   Hardy's moon-wraith casts her cold eye on him in another of his *Satires of Circumstance*, 'The Moon Looks In' (321):

I

I have risen again,
And awhile survey
By my chilly ray
Through your window-pane
Your upturned face,
As you think, 'Ah—she
Now dreams of me
In her distant place!'

The irony here is more clearly circular. The poet, speaking with the voice of his elevated imagination words that his earthbound self (on the other side of the window) cannot hear, enunciates a human hope no doubt prompted by the sight of his tutelary goddess. The new moon seen through glass—a traditional omen of misfortune—has for Hardy associations similar to that of the moon seen over water, preparing his reader, in this instance, for what her beam will reveal when she pierces the blind and the mind of his *princesse lointaine*: a dream of others she is about to meet.

Won't the men be sweet,
And the women sour!

The poet's masochistic imagination removes his image from her mind, transferring to her a coldness she will transfer to him in completion of the inevitable circuit.

The fullest treatment of this theme is to be found in Hardy's 1917 collection, *Moments of Vision*, the first and title-poem (352) of which addresses itself to the question:

> That mirror
> Which makes of men a transparency,
> Who holds that mirror
> And bids us such a breast-bare spectacle see
> Of you and me?

Each succeeding stanza also poses a question, and the poem offers no answers, although we learn more about the nature of the mirror: that its 'magic penetrates like a dart', and that it 'Works well in these night hours of ache', revealing (by moonlight?) tincts never seen by day.

Other 'moments of vision' are more explicit. In 'The Pedigree' (390), the speaker is bent over his family tree 'in the deep of night', a phrase whose submarine connotations are confirmed when

> The uncurtained panes of my window-square let in the watery
> light
> Of the moon in its old age:
> And green-rheumed clouds were hurrying past where mute and
> cold it globed
> Like a drifting dolphin's eye seen through a lapping wave.

The moon, aged as befits the imaginative eye of a seventy-seven-year-old poet, regards him as coldly as the moon-eyed fishes had peered at the submerged *Titanic*, and in very similar terms. Once more the ominous conjunction of moon, water, and window-square portends coldness in love. 'So, scanning my sire-sown tree' (and the unidentified subject leaves one wondering which is the scanner), speaker and/or moon study 'the hieroglyphs of this spouse tied to that'. The ties and tangles of generations as mismatched as the poet's own 'twist into a seared and cynic face', that directs his attention to the window. 'It was a mirror now', reflecting in his own face the centuries' accumulation of searing experience and consequent cynicism. Behind his own face he sees, as down the 'long perspective' of 'the big brass telescope that had been handed on in the family' (*Life*, p. 28), his forbears defined in terms of their relationship with him, his 'begetters ... All with the kindred look'; 'kindred' meaning both familial and similar. The searing and cynicism resulting from the experience of reduplicating the species are themselves so invariably reduplicated as to become family features. In the glass of the mirror/telescope he sees already portrayed his own every thought and word, and *sunk* in the depths of despair as 'in the deep of night', he is forced to the bitter admission:

> 'I am merest mimicker and counterfeit!—
>   Though thinking, *I am I*,
>   *And what I do I do myself alone.*'
> —The cynic twist of the page thereat unknit
> Back to its normal figure, having wrought its purport wry,
> . . .

His confession breaks the spell. The face in the page vanishes as the mirror vanishes in the window-square, leaving only the moon, whose visage is now seen to be stained—presumably with the reflected blood[5] and tears of the suffering generations she has spied upon.

The moon delivers as cold a message in 'Honeymoon Time at an Inn' (466), where again she appears ominously 'at the window-square'. For Hardy and his contemporaries, the word honeymoon would have had its original meaning—that of love's full moon about to wane—and Selene's coming is attended by intimations of frigidity and infidelity, 'At the shiver of morning, a little before the false dawn'. Whereas she had appeared in 'old age' to the peruser of the pedigree, she is now 'in deformed decay' and a victim of brutal mutilation: 'The curve hewn off her cheek as by an adze'. This violence calls attention to the secondary meaning of 'shiver' when the stanza's first line is claustrophobically repeated as its fifth.

The moon's 'speechless eying reached across the chamber', and the speaker, whose voyeuristic eye she is, finds speech for what she sees:

> two souls opprest,
> One a white lady sighing, 'Why am I sad!'
> To him who sighed back, 'Sad, my Love, am I!'

Only the moon-blanched whiteness of the lady distinguishes her from the man who echoes her, as their momentarily single and indivisible 'large-pupilled vision swept the scene'. Then something—and the narrator, reflecting the couple's initial ignorance, does not immediately specify what—

> fell sheer, and crashed, and from the floor
> Lay glittering at the pair with a shattered gaze,
> While their large-pupilled vision swept the scene there,
> And the many-eyed thing outleant.

At what should be a human being's moment of supreme harmony and union, singleness is smashed to jagged multiplicity. The cyclopean eye of the pier-glass, containing 'the eyes of the countless dead who had smirked at it' as the page-glass of the pedigree contained the faces of the poet's begetters, is shattered, shivered, seemingly by the basilisk gaze of the moon. The resemblance to the central symbol of 'The Pedigree' is clear, but the physical violence of hewn cheek and shattered gaze introduces a new element. No more eyes will wear away the mirror's silver, reduplicating themselves, and we wonder whether this image might not betoken an end to reduplication—in a word, sterility. At all events, the bride is more concerned than the groom and 'like a moth skimmed forth', recalling Hardy's earlier poem 'Something Tapped' (396), in which the speaker's vision of his Beloved's face at the window proves, on investigation, to be 'Only a pallid moth, alas'. As the white lady kneels to gather the fragments, the bridegroom reveals his ignorance of what has happened and what it signifies, saying: 'Let it stay where it lies!' For him *it* is still single, and four lines later he tries to reassure her, denying the truth of the portent:

> 'Long years of sorrow this means!' breathed the lady
> As they retired. 'Alas!'
> And she lifted one pale hand across her eyes.
> 'Don't trouble, Love; it's nothing,' the bridegroom said.

That uplifted hand may be a gesture of simple weariness, but it seems more likely that the woman is at once warding off the moon's intrusive beam and blocking its vision of the future: division where they had looked for union, coldness where they had looked for warmth. At this point the poet, whose past was that future, boldly introduces a tragic chorus, the Spirits Ironic and the Spirits of Pity, who offer their antiphonal commentary from 'behind the wainscot'. However, while it is hard to remember that the moon's gaze in this poem is Hardy's gaze, it is hard to forget that the Spirits Ironic speak his lines, and hard to be convinced by the universal law he draws from his own experience. One reader, at least, is left with a troubling sense that Hardy, like Aesop's fox that lost its tail, is anxious to reduplicate the mutilation of his own hopes, to impose his own frigidity and sterility on the loves of others.

Some sense of this might account for the guilt underlying one of the later moments of vision, 'I Looked Up from my Writing' (509), which follows the now familiar pattern:

> I looked up from my writing,
>   And gave a start to see,
> As if rapt in my inditing,
>   The moon's full gaze on me.

The secondary meaning of the second line is revealing of the truth that, not until the moon has entered the poet's room (through the window) and caught his eye, does he 'start to see'. From that moment, she is indeed rapt in his inditing as he is wrapped in her light. To the 'meditative misty head' that illuminates and reflects his own he says, involuntarily, being in a state of semi-hypnotic possession: 'What are you doing there?' And as he sees through her gaze, so she replies through his lips:

> Oh, I've been scanning pond and hole
>   And waterway hereabout
> For the body of one with a sunken soul
>   Who has put his life-light out.

> Did you hear his frenzied tattle?

'Tattle' seems a heartless word to describe the grief of a father who has lost his son on the Western Front, but we ascribe it to the cold eye cast by the moon 'on life, on death', until we remember that the moon is but the poet's telescope and he both scanner and speaker. The 'inditing' of line 3 now emerges as a bitter pun: inditer, turned indicter, turns the beam that has been searching 'pond and hole/And waterway' for the suicide

> Into the blinkered mind
> Of one who wants to write a book
>   In a world of such a kind.

The self-accused moves out of the moon's sight, fearing that unless he interrupts the moment of vision, he may be required to reduplicate the suicide's despairing act. Rather than be called to quench 'his life-light' in a moonlit pond, he eclipses the light of his imagination in a darkened page.

So ends the section of 'Poems of War and Patriotism', and the moon that has initiated so many of Hardy's moments of vision presides over the two poems of the book's 'Finale'. First, in 'The Coming of the End' (510), she rises ominously as ever over water:

> It came to an end;
> Yes, the outgazing over the stream,
> With the sun on each serpentine bend,
> Or, later, the luring moon-gleam;
> It came to an end.

Finally, the poet projects himself to a point in time after the end has come. In 'Afterwards' (511), *after* his *words* have been stilled, he imagines the neighbours 'Watching the full-starred heavens' from their open doors, as he watched them from his window. Because he cannot conceive that, in his absence, his imaginative double will rise, he asks:

> Will this thought rise on those who will meet my face no more,
> 'He was one who had an eye for such mysteries'?

He was not to be stilled, however, for another ten years, and his tutelary goddess continued to preside over poem after poem, one of them shedding a retrospective light on some that had gone before. The dire conjunction of moon and pond is again encountered in 'At Rushy Pond' (680):

> On the frigid face of the heath-hemmed pond
> There shaped the half-grown moon . . . .
>
> And I cared not for conning the sky above
> Where hung the substant thing,
> For my thought was earthward sojourning
> On the scene I had vision of.

The poet does not 'con' the sky, as 'the old moon conned the chamber' in 'Honeymoon Time at an Inn'. Instead, his eye is drawn to the moon's reflection in the pond, as in the earlier poem his moon-gaze had searched out the pier-glass. His vision now is not of 'the eyes of the countless dead', but of one woman wooed beside this water 'in a secret year'. That secrecy, prompted one must suppose by guilt, may account for the veil of euphemism drawn over the penultimate stanza. The speaker seems to imply that the woman died, but his metaphor might be taken to mean that she was simply disappointed in love, grew pale, and withdrew. The initial ambiguity resides in 'the last weak love-words' of line 17, a phrase that causes the reader to wonder whether the weakness refers to the diminished affection of the man or to the deathbed weakness of the woman. The answer is probably both; his coldness having wrecked her 'bloomage' and made white what had been red. Ice, once again, has triumphed over fire, moon over sun.

This poem of the 1920s bears an interesting resemblance to one written more than fifty years earlier that seems to show an intermediate stage in the development of these symbols. 'Neutral Tones' (9) opens:

> We stood by a pond that winter day,
> And the sun was white, as though chidden of God,

and ends with its features reassembled in such a way as to suggest their superimposition one upon another:

> Your face, and the God-curst sun, and a tree,
> And a pond edged with greyish leaves.

The coldness of this pond derives from the season rather than the moon, but the sun that one would expect to be red or gold is white, as if it too were cold, frozen by God's rebuke. Male and female symbols of sun and pond prepare for the mirrored eyes of man and woman, searching for answers to riddles tedious because so often repeated, as their lips discuss the related question: 'which lost the more by our love'.

In the last stanza the past is exchanged for the present, the poet having learnt in the interim 'lessons that love deceives, / And wrings with wrong'. These lessons are said to have 'shaped' the concluding montage of face, sun, tree, and pond. The pun in w/rings leaves no doubt that the shape is circular, or that the reduplicative pattern of so many subsequent 'lunar' poems underlies this too. The 'God-curst' sun, symbolic of the poet, transmits coldness to the woman that he loved, or thought he loved, for Hardy's Well-Beloved can only be adored at a distance.

It is one thing to identify such a reduplicative Figure in the Carpet, but quite another to account for it. The facts of Hardy's life, however, appear to yield some relevant clues. Until he was twenty-five—only two years before writing 'Neutral Tones'—he still considered entering the Church. His most recent and most persuasive biographer believes his subsequent loss of faith to be connected with the influence of a woman,[6] and it would seem that when the omnipotent, male God of his fathers was deposed, a principal contender for the empty throne was a female figure constant only in inconstancy. Like the male contenders, she has various forms and names. In 'The Convergence of the Twain', she is the Spinner of the Years; in 'A Philosophical Fantasy' (884), she is

> Sir or Madam,
> (I know no more than Adam,
> Even vaguely, what your sex is,—
> Though feminine I had thought you
> Till seers as 'Sire' besought you;—
> And this my ignorance vexes
> Some people not a little,
> And, though not me one tittle,
> It makes me sometimes choose me
> Call you 'It', if you'll excuse me?)

Most often, however, it seems as if God the Sun has been replaced by the moon goddess apostrophized in 'At Moonrise and Onwards' (517):

> O Lady of all my time,
> Veering unbid into my view
>   Whether I near Death's mew,
>   Or Life's top cyme!

From being the 'tutelary goddess' in whose likeness Hardy perceived he had been made, she became his 'wraith', the eye of his imagination. 'Selene he *cherished*'—his verb suggesting an active fostering of love—because, unlike Aphrodite whom he feared, she made none of the physical demands on him that he could not meet. Instead, she comes to the window that protects him from the touch of the world and frames the visions that she brings. Alternatively, her telescopic lens will bring him to the outside of a window framing a love-scene within. There are three such scenes in *Human Shows*: 'On the Esplanade' (682), 'In Sherborne Abbey' (726), and 'At a Pause in a Country Dance' (747). In each, there are intimations of approaching grief, as the cold eye of the poet contemplates the prospect of ardour about to cool. The element of erotic satisfaction that he derives from such moments of moonlit vision, implicit in many poems, becomes explicit in one of the most haunting of *Winter Words*, 'Concerning Agnes' (862):

> I am stopped from hoping what I have hoped before—
> Yes, many a time!—
> To dance with that fair woman yet once more
> As in the prime
> Of August, when the wide-faced moon looked through
> The boughs at the faery lamps of the Larmer Avenue.

Tenderly the moon illuminates that evening in 1895 when he danced with Agnes Grove, before turning its gaze from past warmth to the cold present it foretold:

> Yes. She lies white, straight, features marble-keen,
> Unapproachable, mute, in a nook I have never seen.
>
> There she may rest like some vague goddess, shaped
> As out of snow;
> Say Aphrodite sleeping; or bedraped
> Like Kalupso;
> Or Amphitrite stretched on the Mid-sea swell,
> Or one of the Nine grown stiff from thought. I cannot tell!

The poet's imagination luxuriates in the contemplation of Agnes dead, as Pierston's had in the prospect of Avice the first, 'moonlight irradiating her winding-sheet'. There is no mistaking his sensual satisfaction at seeing Aphrodite in thrall to Selene.

With one important exception, Hardy's imaginative processes follow the romantic variation of the platonic pattern that M. H. Abrams identifies in Goethe's *Die Leiden des jungen Werthers*: 'The divine Idea beamed from God into the soul's mirror, thence to be projected on the written page, has become one with the erotic fantasies and fevered emotions of the artist-hero of the *Sturm Und Drang*.'[7] The exception is that, for Hardy, the source of the beam is not God but the moon goddess who has replaced

Him. So closely does her vassal poet identify with her that, seeing his face reflected in hers, he regards her as his wraith.

Pierston at his mirror had seen 'history in his face ... his brow was not the blank page it had once been'; an association of mirror, face, and page found also in 'The Burghers':

> on we prest
> Before a mirror, in whose gleam I read
> Her beauty, his,—and mine own mien unblest.

In 'The Pedigree', the tangled lines of the chronicler's page 'winked and tokened towards the window', where in the moon's mirror the poet finds reflected his ancestral face, and is only released from the Mage's enchantment when he has drawn that face in his own page. So, in 'I Looked Up from my Writing', the poet encounters the hypnotic eye of the moon, and is only able to escape from the revelation it brings

> Of one who wants to write a book
> In a world of such a kind

when he has *written* his own *indictment*, mirrored in his page his face for all to see. Self-revelation may be painful, but for Hardy as for most poets the alternative is a blank page, death-in-life. In 'The Burghers', the husband watching his faithless wife and her lover is 'blanked by such love', until the moon rescues him from eclipse. Similarly, in 'The Going' (277), the bereaved poet tells the absent Emma that he scans the garden's 'alley of bending boughs' for her familiar figure,

> Till in darkening dankness
> The yawning blankness
> Of the perspective sickens me!

The blankness that has swallowed her threatens him: 'I seem like a dead man held on end / To sink down soon'. To recover and reassert his 'sinking' identity he turns to a blank page where soon his image, freshly defined, will rise to the surface. Hardy's pages are mirrors, which the reader at his shoulder reads, as they were written, by moonlight, the radiance of the wraith that triumphantly survives the failures of the flesh.

NOTES

1. All page references are to *The Well-Beloved* (1897), except when stated to the contrary.
2. See Robert Gittings, *Thomas Hardy's Later Years* (1978), p. 88.
3. *Illustrated London News*, 26 November 1892, p. 674. Dr. Mary Jacobus, to whom I am endebted for many insights into Hardy's poetry and prose, calls my attention to Jude's similar obeisance:

> The sun was going down, and the full moon was rising simultaneously behind the woods in the opposite quarter. His mind had become so impregnated with the poem ['*Carmen Saeculare*'] that, in a moment of the same impulsive emotion which years before had caused him to kneel on the ladder, he stopped the horse, alighted, and glancing round to see that nobody was in sight, knelt down on the roadside bank with open book. He turned first to the shining goddess, who seemed to look so softly and so critically at his doings, then to the disappearing luminary on the other hand, as he began:
>
> 'Phoebe silvarumque potens Diana!'
>
> (*Jude the Obscure*, New Wessex ed., 1974, p. 53.)

4. *Illustrated London News*, 1 October 1892, p. 425.
5. At significant moments in Hardy's poems the moon takes the colour of blood. For example, before 'The Church-Builder' (139) hangs himself he notices that 'The rich red windows dim the moon'; and at the end of 'A Trampwoman's Tragedy', 'The red moon low declined'.
6. Robert Gittings, *Young Thomas Hardy* (1975), p. 93.
7. M. H. Abrams, *The Mirror and the Lamp* (1953), p. 44.

Notes on Contributors

PATRICIA CLEMENTS teaches modern literature at the University of Alberta. She has written on modern poetry and nineteenth-century French and English literature. She is preparing, with Robert Merrett, a collection of critical essays on the work of E. M. Forster, and she is working on a study of Walter Pater. She has also published under the name of Gallivan.

CORNELIA COOK is Lecturer in English at Queen Mary College in the University of London. She is author of a book on Joyce Cary, which will be published by Vision Press, and she is working on a critical biography of George Meredith.

ROSEMARY EAKINS was educated at McGill and Oxford, where she has taught nineteenth-century English literature. She has written on Browning and Hardy. She lives in New York, where she is a director of an independent firm of research associates.

SIMON GATRELL is a graduate of St. Edmund College, Oxford. He has compiled, with T. Bareham, a *Bibliography of the Writings of George Crabbe* (1976), and he has written a number of essays on Hardy. He lectures in English at the New University of Ulster.

JULIET GRINDLE is a graduate of Oxford University. She has worked in publishing and she has lectured in English at University College, Cardiff. She has done a critical edition of *Tess of the d'Urbervilles* and she has written on *The Mayor of Casterbridge*.

ISOBEL GRUNDY is Senior Lecturer in English at Queen Mary College, London University. She has published on Pope, Fielding, and Lady Mary Wortley Montagu, whose *Essays and Poems* she edited jointly with Robert Halsband (OUP, 1977). She grew up in Wessex.

PATRICIA INGHAM is Fellow and Tutor in English at St. Anne's College, Oxford. She has published articles on Hardy's fiction, and she is one of the editors of *A Chaucer Glossary* (OUP, 1979).

RONALD MARKEN has taught English at the University of Saskatchewan, Saskatoon, since 1966. He has written articles on Blake, Hopkins, Hardy's fiction and Yeats. He has edited an anthology of prison writing, *Don't Steal This Book*, and published a small volume of his own poems, *Dark Honey*. He teaches modern British poetry, modern drama, prosody, and Irish literature and is working on a book-length study of Yeats's prosody.

S. C. NEUMAN teaches modern literature at the University of Alberta. She has written on autobiography and W. B. Yeats, and her *Gertrude Stein: Autobiography and the Problem of Narration* appeared in the ELS Monograph Series, 1979. She is a founding member of the NeWest Press, Edmonton.

JON STALLWORTHY has written five collections of poems, the most recent being *A Familiar Tree* (1978), and two critical studies, *Between the Lines: W. B. Yeats's Poetry in the Making* (1963) and *Vision and Revision in Yeats's Last Poems* (1969). His biography, *Wilfred Owen* (1974), won the Duff Cooper Memorial Prize, the W. H. Smith & Son Literary Award, and the E. M. Forster Award. He has edited *The Penguin Book of Love Poetry* (1974) and, with Peter France, translated *Alexander Blok: The Twelve and Other Poems* (1970). He now divides his time between an Oxfordshire farmhouse and Cornell University, where he is Anderson Professor of English Literature.

JEREMY STEELE read English and Classics at Oxford, and then worked as an editor for a number of British publishers. Since moving to Australia he has spent most of his time in research at the University of Sydney. His Ph.D. thesis is entitled 'Hardy's Debt to the Classical World'.

GLEN WICKENS teaches English at the University of Alberta. He received his B.A. from the University of British Columbia and his M.A. and Ph.D. from the University of Western Ontario and is the author of articles on Hardy and Tennyson.

Index

Q5